PRIMARY CHILDREN LEARN AT CHURCH

PRIMARY CHILDREN
LEARN AT CHURCH

ETHEL L. SMITHER

Printed for

THE

LEADERSHIP TRAINING PUBLISHING ASSOCIATION

by

ABINGDON PRESS

New York • Nashville

PRIMARY CHILDREN LEARN AT CHURCH

Copyright MCMXLIV by Whitmore & Stone

Library of Congress Catalog Card Number: 44-8719

R

SET UP, PRINTED, AND BOUND BY THE
PARTHENON   PRESS,   AT   NASHVILLE,
TENNESSEE, UNITED STATES OF AMERICA

To my good friends
the Primary girls and boys whom I have taught
this book is dedicated with affection

EDITORS' INTRODUCTION

"THE curriculum is ninety per cent teacher." If this statement is true, the development of a consecrated and skilled staff of leaders is the first responsibility of a teaching church. Too often better materials in the hands of untrained leaders have produced disappointment and discouragement. The equipping of leaders for their teaching task must parallel the introduction of improved types of curriculums. The denominational boards of Christian education are therefore laying great stress upon the development of a qualified leadership.

The total program of leadership education carried forward by these denominations, severally and co-operatively, includes, in addition to a variety of unstandardized and informal programs and materials, the Standard Leadership Curriculum with its three levels or series of courses. Each series has its distinct purpose and field. The Second Series Courses, for which this text is prepared, "are for persons who have a definite interest in leadership education and who are ready for somewhat more extensive work than is involved in the First Series Courses." Each course covers not less than ten fifty-minute periods. Each student, in order to receive a Second Certificate of Progress, must complete ten Second Series Courses, properly distributed, and also fulfill certain requirements as to religious growth, leadership experience, and educational activity.

In making available for these Second Series Courses texts which are educationally sound and relatively inexpensive, the Leadership Training Publishing Association is rendering a unique service. Through its various committees this co-operative publishing group selects writers, circulates outlines and manuscripts for careful criticism, and publishes those which meet the high requirements of the present-day leadership-education program. The books already published are evidence of the past success and present standing of the Association.

7

This text, PRIMARY CHILDREN LEARN AT CHURCH, will replace the former book by the same author, *Teaching Primaries in the Church School*. This new text is intended as a guide and source book for students pursuing Course 241b, "Guiding the Religious Growth of Primary Children" (Teaching Procedures), which is one of the required specialization units for leaders in the Primary Department. It sets forth a high standard in methods and at the same time presents them in a way which is plain to the average church-school teacher. The content is more than a body of reading matter, for it has been written from a wide experience of teaching Primary boys and girls. The book includes many suggestions which are intended to enrich leadership courses and to stimulate thinking, observation, and practical activity on the part of Primary leaders.

The author, Miss Ethel L. Smither, has had excellent training in undergraduate and graduate schools of education. Her experience in public-school teaching, in field service, and as an editor of church-school publications for children in the Methodist Church has given her a wealth of background from which to write. She is a proficient author, having written a number of books for children as well as several for children's workers.

The Leadership Training Publishing Association, confident of the widespread use and approval of this text, recommends it to those who wish to become skillful leaders of Primary children.

For the Leadership Training Publishing Association,

ERWIN L. SHAVER, *Chairman*

J. S. ARMENTROUT, *Chairman,*
Editorial-Educational Committee

ATHA S. BOWMAN, *Chairman,*
Committee on Children's Division Texts

FOREWORD

PRIMARY CHILDREN LEARN AT CHURCH has been written to help Primary teachers guide the religious growth of the children for whom they are responsible. It seeks to state clear and definite purposes. Then the book should help teachers to see the children. The whole child is kept in mind; for religion is a part of a child's entire life, and all of it is involved in any religious learning.

One aim is to help teachers to see how important their own Christian experience is to their children. Religion is made manifest in life to young learners. What the teachers say is colored inevitably by what they are. The spiritual aspects of religion make their impress on children supremely through the teachers' experience of God and the Living Christ, so the effectiveness of all their teaching is based on what they are. In this sense all members of the adult congregation teach the children of their church.

This book deals with the materials for religious education and the methods for their use. Teaching children at church is a challenging task and privilege when the teacher makes good preparation and knows rich materials and many methods for their use with children. The individual interests and differences of children can then be met by their religious teachers.

Constant emphasis is placed upon the need for parents and teachers to work along with the children, for their unity is essential to any successful learning experience at church. Unless the child's life at home lends further meaning to his church learnings, the latter are likely to be vague and ineffective. For these reasons, parents must be included in all plans of the Primary Department. Most parents are eager to work with teachers when they grow convinced that the church-school worker is genuinely in earnest about the re-

9

ligious life of the child, anxious to help him grow, and understanding of his needs and abilities.

Worship is central in all learning that is religious, for through worship life establishes its relation to God. Purposes become religious when fellowship with God is related to them. Work and activity gains religious meaning through related worship. The book not only shows how learning and teaching should be associated with the worship of the entire Primary group, but it emphasizes the worship experience of small group or class. Worship, of course, has little meaning for young children until there is this unity of experience.

This book really is a record of experiences with Primary children through the years. It also reflects many opportunities that I have had to know and counsel with Primary teachers. It is written for the great group of leaders in our churches whom I have watched as they worked patiently, devotedly, and often unnoticed, to make religion a reality and a center of life for Primary children. These workers have come a long way in their improved preparation for the task. If this book inspires them to go ahead in their teaching and if it furnishes suggestions that lead to greater skill in their work, it will accomplish its purpose.

ETHEL L. SMITHER

Richmond, Virginia

CONTENTS

CONTENTS

14

Chapter 1

WHAT ARE THE PURPOSES OF PRIMARY LEADERS IN THE CHURCH?

The Primary group. The Primary leader reaches the church early on this Sunday morning. For the first time in her teaching life she has arrived before any child puts in his appearance. Her preparations are made; materials for work are ready. She can give her attention to the six-, seven and eight-year-olds who make up the Primary group. Here they come. John has run so hard that his golden, fine-spun hair lies damp on his forehead. He has . new book to show. "And I can read it, too," he announces proudly. Mabel brings Jean, her six-year-old sister. Jean smile. at the teacher but says nothing. Mabel tells of their plans for the afternoon. Mabel is eight and responsible—too much so for Jean's good, for she dominates her. The children come by twos and threes. Sometimes they are brought by a parent who has a plan to suggest or a question to ask. Last of all, ten minutes after work has begun, Vera enters, a large doll in her arm., an expression of "No, you can't hold her" in her brown eyes.

The Primary children and their teachers are at church. Why have they come? The leaders have foregone a leisurely Sunday breakfast. The parents have made the greater effort to bring their boys and girls. What do the adults of the church—pastor, parents, teachers, and church leaders—hope to accomplish for these children?

Goals for religious guidance grow out of at least three elements in the life of any church group. First, they are the religious heritage, faith, and experience of congregation, communion, and neighborhood. The adults in any Christian church wish to share with the growing life of the congregation their knowledge, experience, and conviction.

13

Second, the trends of the times make a genuine difference in what is emphasized in religious guidance. Mature adults who have lived through the rapid changes of the last two decades realize how powerful an influence the times exert on both teaching and preaching. So religious teaching, when it has power, is colored by what is going on in the world. Third, the adult's understanding of the needs and maturities of the children determines materials and plans that are used that group and individual may be guided in religious knowledge, activity, and insight.

A knowledge of all three of the factors that have been discussed is necessary before wise and comprehensive purposes can be chosen. The religious beliefs, faith, and experience of the congregation and communion and the needs of the times largely determine what values to emphasize. A knowledge of children decides when and how to teach the content that is considered of importance.

A view of the children. An understanding of child nature is of supreme importance to any person who wishes to help children to continue to grow religiously. So teachers ask themselves many questions about the children. How mature are they? This is another way of asking, What are they ready and able to learn and to do? How do they learn? Under what conditions do they live in home, community, and school? What daily problems do they face? The teacher respects the problems of children. She knows that if they are left unsolved they can retard religious development.

Primary teachers know that children lead no rosy, irresponsible lives. Childhood has its struggles, fears, difficulties, and disappointments as truly as adulthood. When the teacher keeps confidential records of her pupils, she finds each one of them bristling with problems. Some of these problems are a sense of insecurity, a desire to be considered big or important, a desire to cling to babyhood, unhappiness over failure, confusion about acceptable ways of behaving, and terror at the thought of death. Questions about God, the nature of the universe, the meaning of life, will be listed. "I waked up early," George told his teacher. "I thought and

I thought. I thought about breathing and would I keep on breathing. It made me scared." The more the teacher knows about Primary children and about the individuals whom she teaches, the better prepared is she to set up important purposes for their religious guidance.

Primary leaders study their children in order to provide the environment and guidance that will help them to grow wholesomely and steadily. The teacher must patiently and reverently proceed at the rate of the children's development. The first thing that Primary teachers learn about the children is that there are wide differences in maturity between the six- and the eight-year-olds. As the teacher watches the children, she learns that in most Primary groups the children are in general at two levels of maturity. Those six and seven years of age are in one. The eight-year-olds and the nine-year-olds, who at present are usually grouped with older Juniors, have reached another stage of growth. How to help the younger children and at the same time guide the eight-year-olds is the problem of the Primary leaders in many churches. The teacher learns that maturation refers to a stage of *oldness,* not to age in terms of birthdays. Some children of six or seven or eight are six, seven, or eight physically, mentally, socially, and emotionally as well as in years. Others at any of these ages may be three years old or four, or five, or nine, or ten, in some phases of their development. Some are nine or ten mentally but only five or six socially.

Jack is an example of the bundle of maturities and immaturities that are found in almost every child. He is eight years old and in the second grade at school. He reads with early fourth-grade ability. He has a wider range of information than most children in the sixth grade. The interests of many of the other children seem annoyingly babyish to him. He is a tall boy and of normal weight. His muscular co-ordinations are poor. He cannot skip or run so well as many five-year-old children.

Socially, Jack is just learning how to get along with other children, and he has a deep feeling of social insecurity.

Sometimes he spends his playtime chasing the other boys and girls with a stick. At other times he tries to stay with the teacher and seems afraid of the boys. He is constantly trying to do and say funny things to attract attention.

Religiously, Jack shows many fears. He is blindly trying to find the meaning of the universe, of God, of his own life. Often he torments himself with religious ideas that he is too immature to grasp. Every child in every group or class in the Primary Department is just such a challenging combination of uneven maturities.

Children have a rate of growth that is sometimes rapid and sometimes slow. A child may seem to make no progress for a long time and then spurt ahead. Each child needs help that he may take what is the next step religiously for him. Yet a knowledge of what Primary children are like in general helps the teacher to help the individual. The common oldnesses of children at six and seven years and, in turn, of the eight-year-olds can be used by their teachers as aids in understanding them and in planning for group living and learning in the church school.

THE YOUNGER PRIMARY CHILD

Need for security. Children of six and seven years of age go through a time when they charge from younger to older childhood. They gradually grow accustomed to public-school life and its demands. The changes that they face increase their need of security in their widening world. Unless they have confidence in their new ways of living and adjust happily to them, they will not continue to make that free, direct attack on their problems that is fundamental to wholesome character growth and religious development. Children who are too quiet and "good" are the ones who need special help. They feel too insecure to be themselve in the new surroundings, and so their growth is hindered.

The bases of security of the younger child must be extended to the wider social relations that boys and girls of Primary age have. Kindly, dependable parents and a home of their own were the most important earlier sources of a sense of security. Now the friendliness and the at-easeness of the teacher are important in encouraging a sense of belonging at public school and at church. Homelike surroundings and chances for normal child activity help also. The teacher's deep sense of religious values and her fellowship with God, more than any other factors, make the church truly a religious place for the children.

Primary children need at first to have the mother relationship extended to the school. Later in the period this attitude to the teacher should be outgrown. A sense of belonging to the group replaces it. The Primary teacher who has long and happy experience with younger Primary children has many children unconsciously call her "Mother." They depend on her presence, steadiness, friendliness, and wisdom when they make new ventures. And who knows how important a part this faith in parent and teacher has in laying foundations for the child's faith and trust in God?

Undeveloped social sense. The six- and seven-year-olds are so undeveloped socially that their self-absorption is only slightly diluted by any sense of "otherness." One of the best pictures of this quality of young child life is shown in this poem:

SPILLING

When Earth goes turning over,
I should not mind at all
If half a little river
Should tip itself and fall;
Or half a little ocean
Or half a little sea.
I'd rather Earth would spill them all
Than to spill *me*.[1]

Of course, many children at six years of age have had such valuable fellowship with socially minded adults that they are far beyond six or seven socially. But in general the six- or seven-year-old is just beginning to learn that other

[1] Kathryn Worth, *Story Parade*, September, 1939, p. 34.

children find joy in the same things that make him happy and that what hurts him hurts another child. He is just beginning to think in terms of "we" as well as "I" and "me." That God is no respecter of persons but is just and all-inclusive in love is an idea that must depend for comprehension on this growth of a sense of tender regard for others, an ability to imagine how others feel. The more protected the child is, usually the less mature is his "we" feeling toward other children. One of the tasks of the Primary teacher is to help the younger children to think, purpose, and find satisfaction in widening circles of social living. She can be sure that this is the very essence of religious teaching. We read in the First Epistle of John, "He who will not love his brother whom he has seen, cannot possibly love the God whom he has never seen"; [2] and we recall the second of the Two Great Commandments.

In the here and now. Children of six years live in the present with no sense of history and vague ideas of time and space. The seven-year-olds take the first simple steps out into a larger understanding. The words "day," "week," "month" begin to have real meaning. Learning to tell time and to know the day of the week and the month of the year comes at this age. A seven-year-old said triumphantly, "I said all the days of the week over to myself. Nobody helped me." The teacher asked the other children in the class if they knew them too. Only one or two did. This child tries to understand the ways of living that are familiar to him and is confused by a premature introduction to those that are removed in time and space. His ideas of time are usually expressed in terms of when to eat or when to play. This means that religion for the six- and the seven-year-old must be very practical and close to his own life. It must link the familiar things of everyday with a sense of the goodness of God. The child's acts of service should be for people whom he can know and understand. A seven-year-old group were dying Easter eggs. They were to keep some and send

[2] I John 4:20 (Moffatt).

others to a crippled-children's hospital. Ted lingered after the others had gone. He came to the teacher and gave her the yellow egg that he had dyed for himself. "Send it to the crippled children," he said. "I can run." The boy's face was lovely and radiant with his sense of sympathy.

Teachers of younger Primary children cannot expect them to understand long purposing and planning. They plan as they go along. Historical arrangements of material and rich historical backgrounds contribute more confusion than understanding. For example, a series of Bible stories arranged in the order of their appearance in the Bible never carries a time sequence for pupils in the first and second grades. The arrangement may satisfy the teacher, but the children gain no sense of developing history from it.

Children of this age solve problems well and surely, but they think out problems step by step and work out ideas as they go along.

Stating general principles and summarizing what has been learned, except in simplest fashion, has little value for the younger Primary children. Their interests are as wide as their lives, it is true. They often introduce subjects in conversation that reflect their contacts with many advanced problems, but this is no indication that they are ready for serious study in these areas.

Work must be kept simple to be of value to them religiously. One Primary teacher invited a worker at a local mission to tell about the program there. After a very satisfactory time together the leader asked her group, "And what did Miss ——— say that was especially interesting to you?" The answers were of simple, practical, unrelated things. There was no organization of ideas and no statement of principles. The teacher reported that she gained new understanding of children from the incident. First, she realized anew that she must teach in the most specific ways. Second, she learned that the spirit of service and love of God of a devoted Christian can communicate itself to young children and nurture them religiously.

Learning through sensory experience. The six- or

seven-year-old learns by firsthand acquaintance and through
his senses. He understands as he investigates with eyes, ears,
tongue, nose, hands. One of the most rejoicing and worshiping groups of children the writer ever saw were singing:

> I am glad for my nose, and my ears, and my hands
> To smell with, to hear with, to touch.
> I love your beautiful, beautiful world,
> And I love you, God, so much! [8]

They had been using all their senses in a happy learning
time, and the song was a climax of their living.

Learning through social living. Just as they learn from
opportunities to use their senses, younger Primary children
grow through social experiences. Much learning at this age
is implicit; that is, it · an absorption from the social group.
The communication of spirit and devotion from mature
Christians to growing ones is of great importance in religious teaching. The atmosphere of joyous reverence and
faith, the sense of the reality and presence of God that the
adults experience, is fundamental to religious nurture for
the Primary group. The teachings of the Bible have little
meaning until they are learned through living and through
association with adults who have known their truth. So the
Primary children will grow religiously where the church
provides a chance for them to live, work, and play together
and to have fellowship with adults who are devoted Christians. Stories, songs, and verses from the Bible will have
a place in such a Primary Department when they enrich
and lend meaning to the life that goes on there.

How ideas grow. Just think of so homely a word as
mother and of how long it takes for its real meaning to be
enriched by experience. Think also of where the Primary
child is in the process of understanding the complete meaning of the word.[4] Then the teacher will have a better idea

---

[8] From "Thank you, God" by Grace N. Crowell, *Picture Story Paper*, Novem-
ber 26, 1939.

[4] An interesting study of the development of social ideas is Joy M. Lacey,
Social Studies Concepts of Children in the First Three Grades, Bureau of
Publications, Teachers College, Columbia University, 1932.

of what kind of teaching will help or hinder Primary children. Verbalizations, words like honesty or kindness, that classify many ways of acting, or talks about religious qualities or character traits, are highly confusing. The children are not ready for them. They are only beginning to work out the meaning of words in life.

Children do as adults do, feel as they feel, and—if the adults are not careful to help them think for themselves— take their ideas secondhand. They accept ideas of religious values uncritically instead of growing into their own. Children who have taken over thoughtlessly the religious ideas of a past generation may become the adolescents who must break away with pain in order ever to find a faith of their own. Every generation must learn to place its own emphasis on Christian values and to gain new understanding of them. Talking and teaching are not synonymous, for words are after all only names for experience. The more generalized and abstract they are, the less helpful they are to Primary children who need to build, through active living, the background for understanding word or idea. "Children often do not express themselves in conventional form, especially if they do not feel pressure from above; so that the meaning of experience to them must often be felt rather than found expressed in so many words." [5]

Of course, the child sometimes learns the meaning of a particular experience through talking about it. Yet the teacher can talk too much and too soon. It is a revealing exercise for most teachers to check up on just how much they do talk and how little chance the children have to speak. Elizabeth Hubbard found that if her six-year-olds went on a trip on Thursday, she could expect them to begin talking about it on the next Monday, and that if she pressed them too soon for an expression in words, the children's grasp of the experience never developed. "The parents are much interested in young children's reactions to experiences. They tell me

[5] Mary Ross Hall, *Children Can See Life Whole*, Association Press, 1940, p. 146.

that often after family excursions they have asked their children at once about them, and getting no recall, are bewildered and conclude the experience valueless. If they wait as I do, they say that they too are rewarded. We both find that by forcing it too soon we sometimes seem to balk later response." [6] What a significant report this is for the church-school teacher of Primary children.

The younger Primary children need many opportunities for expression other than in words. Some of their surest ways of "speaking" are painting or drawing, building, singing, rhythms. The teacher often finds the key to a child's inner life when he expresses himself.

Literal-mindedness. Primary children do not understand religious ideas that are stated in analogies or by using words in a double sense. One group of seven- and eight-year-olds were listening to a story in which a joke was played. The phrase "my white elephants" was used. Even the brightest children could not catch the double meaning. The teacher explained that white elephants did not necessarily mean elephants, that it was a way of speaking about anything that was a nuisance to a person. Two of the more mature children said in turn, "It means little toy elephants," and, "Maybe they are like the white ones my mother has." Religious symbolisms are even harder to understand. Candles are lights, nothing more. An intangible trait of character cannot be represented meaningfully by some physical object. Jesus, the Light of the World, is an idea that Primary children cannot understand because they do not yet have the ability to make an object stand for a spiritual reality. This limitation often baffles the religious teacher, as the writer well knows.

Religion a part of the entire life. Since the child lives life instead of thinking about it, his religious life is a part of his whole experience, not a phase of it that can be set to one side and developed in one certain place, the church school. Religious education for six- and seven-year-olds

[6] Elizabeth V. Hubbard, *Your Children at School*, John Day Company, 1942, p. 16.

means much more than instruction in ideas of God and of Jesus, in the Bible, in missionary education. For this reason, any plans for Primary children in church school must be quite like their public-school experience if the latter is a good one.

The public-school experience of the Primary child can make a contribution to his religious learning, for a young Primary child is learning to think, to wonder, to live socially, to choose in all his environments. The home is probably more important than either public or church school as a school of religion. Whenever the child seeks meaning for life and wonders about it, senses his own worth, learns to find his life happily in the social group, grows sensitive to the needs and worth of others, learns to bear responsibility for his part of the task, learns to choose the higher rather than the lower value, learns to stick at a worthy task, learns to feel joy and wonder and awe in the presence of beauty and mystery, he is learning religiously.

One second grade kept a weekly record from September to June of the hours of sunrise and sunset. In March it became apparent that the decrease and later the increase in the daily amount of sunlight followed a regular schedule. The children were struck by the fact. One boy said, "It looks just as if God had planned for it." The teacher answered quietly, "I believe he did." Then the group sang one of their favorite prayer hymns, "Lord of the Sunlight." Science and religion hand in hand! For the modern child they must be united if either is to have enriching influence on his life.

THE OLDER PRIMARY CHILD

Broader social outlook. Now look at the eight-year-olds, since the majority of churches still group the six-, seven- and eight-year-olds together. Many of the characteristics of younger children continue. What are some differences that can be noted between older and younger Primary children? First of all, the older children's sense of space and mastery of their own background are so well developed that they can profitably learn to contrast their own way of living with that of other groups. They need to learn of other ways of living, with a special emphasis on the common humanity of people, and to see differences in the light of causes. In this manner they avoid the habit of being too satisfied with their own group's way of life and thought, and they learn not to defend it as the only one. The contrasts should be made in areas of living that are not so strange as to be frightening and repulsive.[7] The younger Primary children have been growing out of the here and now. The eight-year-old boys and girls have entered into the here and there, also. This means that the children are ready to study the customs of Bible times and to be introduced to missionary-education activities that are no longer confined to the child's own community.

Ability to purpose and to think. The older Primary children can organize their own purposes on an increasingly wider basis. Any Primary teacher knows how the lists of questions of six- and seven- and of eight-year-olds vary in length and in scope. It is usually useless to expect first and second grades to list their questions and problems at the beginning of a unit. Eight-year-olds can do it easily.

The eight-year-old is also beginning to organize his thinking. He is conscious of his old ideas as he begins to reorganize and expand them or to reject them as babyish. When the teacher has his confidence, she has a wonderful chance to guide him and to help the child get his first conscious understanding of God, of the meaning of life, and of social relationships. But literal-mindedness is still a great limitation.

Three examples of how eight-year-olds are thinking may be given:

The first shows how easily children can assume a provincial attitude toward God. Joan and Betty, both eight years old, were matching "samples" one day. In the midst of the play an adult heard Betty say, "You know the Jews are God's chosen people."

"I don't believe it," answered Joan hotly.

"Well, you ask Aunt Kate," answered Betty. "Aren't the Jews God's chosen people?"

Aunt Kate said, "The Jews believed that God had chosen them for a special task. They were his special people and he was their God."

"Do you believe that?" asked Joan.

"No," was the reply. "I think that God has no special people. Wherever men love him and each other and try to obey him, they are God's children."

"Well, that is wrong," Joan insisted. "God ought to have a chosen people. The Americans ought to be it."

The following incident shows how eight-year-olds are struggling to think of God in terms of the world they know and so are growing toward a spiritual understanding. One Sunday, Charles said, "Why doesn't God come down where we can see him?"

"Where do you think God is?" the teacher asked.

Before Charles could answer, Jack said, "Well, he is not up in the sky. There was a man who went up there, and that is stratosphere."

Immediately several other children volunteered information about the earth's covering of atmosphere and about the stratosphere. The teacher took the first steps in helping them to think of God as spirit, not located in a special place.

Then there is the child who is rejecting, on the basis of reasoning, negative ideas of God that adults have used as threats. Patty said, "My mother says God sees everything I do, so I better be good. I don't believe it. If God watches me all the time, he watches other children, too—and he can't. He couldn't see us all at one time."

The teacher answered, "You are thinking of God like a little child, Patty. As we grow up we do not think of God as having eyes to spy on people. We think of God as in and back of everything that is beautiful and true and powerful and good in the world. Of course, when you are doing or thinking wrong things, you cannot feel near to God; for they are not like God. That is what your mother means, I think. You can see how every child in all the world could feel near to God in that way. They could think of God as like a Father who is interested in what they do."

"O yes, I see," said Patty. "I'll think about it some more."

One could give many other incidents. One of the real needs of the eight-year-old is companionship with an adult who understands the child's ability to grasp fundamental Christian ideas. She need not be afraid of opening the child's mind to difficult ones so long as she gives him something that he can work on at once. He should sense that his quest for God will carry him "beyond the utmost bound of human thought." How much better than blocking child thought by hasty, sweeping answers that seem to explain everything.

Desire to find out for himself. Since the eight-year-old is beginning to read simple materials fairly well, he is interested in books and in reading for himself. Books can help to give him some of the knowledge he needs and aid him in setting up purposes and working them out. He can make brief reports about what he is learning, and he enjoys listening to other children make them. Younger Primary children do not report well or learn much from listening to one another.[8] Older Primaries should have training in the courtesy that is necessary in exchanging ideas.

Child friendships more important. Child friendships begin to be much more important and to last longer. When David entered the third grade, he had two consuming passions: to let Sam know how much he appreciated his witticisms and to keep Donald's adoration. All three boys needed attention if these friendships were to be of value to them. The teacher emphasized steadiness. The four talked about what it meant in terms of practical behavior. Later on David and Sam were having a chat with the teacher. A report had just come in on the height and weight growth of the children, and the teacher told them how they had made progress. "That

[8] See Jean Piaget, *Judgment and Reasoning in the Child*, Harcourt, Brace & Co., 1928.

is not the only way you have grown," she said.

"I know," said David. "I used to laugh at Sam all the time and now I don't."

"I don't think that funny stuff's so hot any more," said Sam.

"Sometimes you say really funny things that we all enjoy," the teacher added, "but you are steadier and do not try to show off all the time." To direct the quality of child friendship for eight-year-olds is a real duty of their teacher. Many of them get into trouble, even to the point of delinquency, because they lack ideas of wholesome group activity.

A keener urge to grow. All children want to grow up and to be respected as persons. At this time they begin to look to adult life for patterns of what they wish to become. This desire to grow expresses itself in a feeling of independence. "Let me do it my own way," pleaded Don when the teacher tried to help him. "I know what I want to do." "Let me read it and find out for myself," asked Gerald. "I like that better than so many stories." If she is wise the teacher becomes guide, comrade, and counselor. She helps the children to help themselves. She does not always give the answer. Often she has to leave an incident incomplete that the children may do their own thinking.

PURPOSES FOR THE RELIGIOUS GUIDANCE OF PRIMARY CHILDREN

After the teacher has studied the children, she asks herself that perplexing question, "What should be my purposes for their religious guidance?" All Christian teachers have the supreme purpose of leading their children so that they become stalwart Christian persons. They want the boys and girls to grow in a knowledge of God and of Jesus. They want the children to love God supremely and to serve him gladly. They hope that the child's entire life will be motivated by Christian faith and trust.

The leaders of children hope that their boys and girls will learn a sense of social responsibility that gradually gains

Christian motivation. The Second Great Commandment teaches that love of one's neighbor is required of the followers of Jesus. As Bishop Herbert Welch once said in a sermon, it takes God and at least two persons to make a Christian. The Primary teacher realizes that her children are just at the point where teaching a sense of responsibility for one's neighbors is of great importance.

Then the teacher knows that perseverance, a form of Christian trust, is required of all who hold a place in the kingdom of God. Jesus spoke warningly of taking one's hand from the plow and of seed of hasty and shallow growth. The Christian teacher knows that not only must she lay foundations for a life centered in God and in companionship with Christ but that to accomplish this she must train children to persevere in good will and in their search for an understanding of God and fellowship with him.

Last, the teacher plans to nurture the religious life of the Primary children by sharing with them her own love and trust in God. She wants them to know her sense of joy in his service.

So far as they are meaningful to the children, she shares with them their religious heritage in the Bible and in the hymns and ritual of the church.

For her convenience, the teacher states her purposes in practical and specific terms. She may divide them into six areas. Of course, in the child's religious learning there are no such arbitrary divisions. The six statements of purpose can be arranged under the following headings:

1. Relationship with God and Ideas of God
2. Relationship with Jesus and Ideas of Jesus
3. The Child and the Church Fellowship
4. The Child's Heritage in the Bible
5. The Child in His Personal Relationships
6. The Child in His Social Relationships.

Relationship with God and ideas of God. "What shall we teach the Primary child of God? What is he mature enough to learn?" are questions that the teacher asks. The Primary children should have a sense of the reality of God and a growing trust in his wisdom and goodness when they enter the department. To the growing knowledge of God as revealed by Jesus, the teacher will contribute in terms of what the children need and can learn. Without companionship with teachers and parents who know and rejoice in their fellowship with God, the teaching of God to Primary children is barren and unmoving. If children have also opportunities to enter into an active life that is loving, friendly, and investigative, and if they have many opportunities to worship and to go without fear to adults when they are puzzled or insecure, the thoughts of God as Father, as the living source of power and of creative good will, gradually emerge. It is the Primary teacher's task to see that the children have a chance for such a church life and to do what she can to help the parents to create such a life for them at home. Later on the children will use what they experience now to organize their growing ideas of God.

Adults are often disturbed because young Primary children express crude and inadequate ideas of God. Some conscientious Christians refrain from the practice of prayer with young children in order to safeguard the child from such first ideas and from the pain of reorganizing them. This seems impossible, and also a narrowing of experience. To keep a little child from praying, one must separate him from worship at home and at church. Probably this limitation of experience would cause more retardation in religious growth than a necessary rethinking as he grows older.

There are other parents and teachers who believe that even little children may avoid crude ideas of God if their parents and teachers are wise. This is a point at which no one should be dogmatic since our best knowledge of child life and its religion is so inadequate. But it seems natural for young children to have crude ideas of God; for their ideas in much simpler realms of thought are inadequate, vague, and often primitive. The more spiritual understanding of God is sensed at this age, not stated. It grows through association with adults who know and worship God as Spirit.

The teacher's task is to see that the child's idea of God keeps pace with his ability to think and to gain insight. A child should expect to reorganize his thought of God over and over again. This should be welcomed as a lifelong adventure of the Christian. The child is harmed, not by crude, early ideas of God, but by the absence of a growing idea of God. The concept of God should always be associated with the highest and best that a child can imagine. Many Primary teachers find that rethinking their own ideas of God and then trying to state them in words that children can understand is a challenging and helpful activity in leading children.

The children's ideas of God grow not only through their association with more mature Christians and through their active church life but also through many experiences with the natural world—with growing things; the seasons; the cycles of growth; the work of wind, water, and sun. All of these experiences will be approached without sentimentality and with scientific knowledge. Sometimes a song, a p em, a devotional passage from the Bible that has been set to music will be used to lift an experience of wonder to the level of worship. Many opportunities for expression in music and the fine arts should be associated with these contacts with nature and with wonder over the meaning of life.

All this is especially true of the eight-year-old. The teacher recalls that he is thinking through and reorganizing his earlier understandings of God. "When I was little," children have confided over and over again, "I thought . . . Now I think . . ." He needs a teacher who will challenge him with an expectation of hard thinking, with a sense of quest. She will not overwhelm him, of course, by expecting him suddenly to become adult in insight. He needs a person whom he can trust and to whom he can take his questions. At times his adult friend needs to say, "I do not know. No one does. This is what I believe. You keep on thinking until you know what you believe. This is what I find in the Bible and in other books that tell about God. This is what Jesus believed about the question that puzzles you."

The eight-year-old has this same need in understanding and practicing prayer. One group was talking about praying at home. The teacher told the story "The Lost Children." [9]

"What kind of prayer do you think Roger prayed?" she asked.

"Now I lay me down to sleep," one child responded thoughtlessly.

"He couldn't," said George. "They were in the woods. They weren't going to sleep!"

Out of this incident grew a judgment that prayer must fit the occasion and be thoughtful.

The eight-year-old can begin to learn that prayers are Christian if they are in accord with Jesus' practice and teaching of prayer. They can learn that vengeful, unintelligent prayers are to be avoided.

Eight-year-olds are often challenged by the idea that God and man are co-workers. "God won't let those children starve," Edna said one day. "He'll take care of them."

"How do you think God works?" the teacher asked. The discussion and prayer that followed led the children toward an acceptance of responsibility for service in the kingdom of God.

Many children will need help in learning how to pray. The prayers of the department group are inadequate in giving the training in prayer that children should have at this age. There should be many times when prayer will occur in the class or smaller group. In the writer's judgment, these and other expressions of worship are the times when the work of the Primary teacher becomes religious. These are the climaxes for which she works through all the other activities of the group.

Relationship with Jesus and ideas of Jesus. The younger Primary children continue to learn of Jesus as one

[9] *The Children's Story Garden*, collected by a Committee of the Philadelphia Yearly Meeting of Friends. J. B. Lippincott Co.

who was interested in all sorts of people. He made them happier and helped them to be well and strong and able to live more fully as children of God. He loved children, and they were glad to have him for their friend. He knew God better than anyone ever has. He helped other people to know God as their Father and to learn to love and serve him with all their hearts.

The older children, in addition, will gain a first simple, connected picture of Jesus—baby, boy, man. They will enjoy learning of his home life and of the customs of Palestine, the country where he lived. This sort of knowledge is more than an understanding of background and custom. It makes Jesus more real for many children. Many of these older children will be glad also they can have a part in the work of the church that is composed of his friends.

The church and the Primary child. The Primary leaders set up an environment at church in which the children feel secure because they feel that they belong. It will be free, dependable, friendly, and full of opportunities to be active, to serve others, to investigate, to experiment, to face problems on childlike levels. Children will have chances for fellowship with adults, at church and in the community, whose lives are actively expressing good will and a conscious relationship of sonship to a Christlike God.

The younger children will learn how to work and care for the church, will take trips of investigation about the church, will have experiences of worship and of active work there.

Parents and teachers work together and counsel together that they may understand each other and that the children may feel a unity in the teachings at home and church.

The same environment will be continued for the eight-year-olds. Their chances to serve at church will be larger ones. Causes for need as well as response to it will be studied. The idea of God as the loving Father of all will be introduced. They will have their first glimpse of the Christian fellowship around the world. More and more the eight-year-old should have chances to participate in congregational worship and in church projects as well as in those of his own group. He will begin to think of the church as a fellowship of the friends of Jesus. In some denominations the children will have their first experience of the sacrament of the Lord's Supper. They will think of it as a way of remembering Jesus.

One important part of the Primary teacher's work is to see that the children plan only so much as they can do. Then she should see that they stick to what they start and finish it. Many church activities thoughtlessly begun and never finished can be of real harm to the child's growing personality.

The minister's friendship means much to Primary children. The writer recalls two ministers who held real places in the affection of the children. The first flowers from their garden went to these friends. The boys and girls would consult them about puzzling questions. The door of the study was always open to the Primary children. Years after these boys and girls remember their friends with love and gratitude.

The child's heritage in the Bible. The teacher will introduce the younger Primary children to a few simple Bible stories, mainly from the New Testament. They will illustrate the way of love and friendliness that Jesus taught and will help them to know him. She will help them to use brief devotional Bible passages in their own expression of wonder and joy. Some of them will be set to music. She shows a genuine interest in the Bible. Church hymns, ritual, and psalter, except for a few selected passages, are too adult for these children.

As we have said, the older children will be given a first connected picture of Jesus. It will be a very simple one. Some of the stories of followers in the Early Church are interesting to older Primary children. They may read some of the great stories of the Old Testament, like the ones of David and Jonathan, of David sparing Saul, and of Nehemiah. They will hear simple Old Testament stories that raise few problems for them. They will enjoy and learn to use certain Bible passages in worship.

They will contrast Bible customs and backgrounds with their own and make a beginning in handling the Bible as a book. Many churches give Bibles to the children at the end of the third grade.

The child in his personal relationships. The teacher has a rare privilege in the guidance of children so that they become strong Christians. The teacher knows that this period marks the years children learn increasingly to think, to choose, and to do for themselves.

The teacher should help the children to understand that certain ways of thinking and acting are in keeping with the Christian life. The children make a beginning in choosing, acting, and judging in the light of religious values.

The teacher tries to help any child who lives under such strain that his development is hindered to find as much release as possible. At times he is helped to find a more constructive way of feeling and acting. When troubles start among the children, the teacher helps them to settle their disputes in pleasant and friendly ways. She helps some children to find release from the tensions that trouble them through joyful work and experiences of beauty, as in music, poetry, art. One child literally had no privacy at home. She loved to sit in a quiet corner and read. She was relaxed and at peace when she left the church.

There are other children whom the teacher helps by working with the parents. Sometimes a change at home is necessary if the child's development is to continue. John had an older brother who tormented him. John in turn pestered younger or weaker children. Though the mother was sure that there was no connection between the two facts, she made certain changes at home that helped to set John more at peace.

Sometimes the child's need is more deepseated and more serious. Alvin's father has an incurable disease. His mother supports the family. The boy is very lonely, for he is lost without her. His eyes pain his teacher, for they are dark wells of unhappiness. He is a constant center of trouble. He fights regularly with the other children. Often he is "crying mad." He talks all the time and moves restlessly. His teacher makes special times to talk to him. She watches a streamliner that he greatly admires, even though it takes extra time. She lends him books to read. She has special work for him to do just with her. Sometimes he works in her garden. She knows that, to help him grow religiously, she must relieve his unhappiness as much as possible.

The Primary teacher best guides children in their personal relationships when she remembers that they are in a state of becoming. She does not expect them to learn Christian graces of living once for all and without effort and many setbacks. The most helpful religious teacher is one who takes the attitude of a physician toward her children. A doctor never condemns a patient for a sudden relapse. He does not label him "bad." The physician continues to ask himself how he can help the patient and so overcome the new difficulty. Wise religious teachers of Primary children take a similar point of view. Labeling a child "bad" only builds up barriers between teacher and child. It fails in Christian tenderness. Teachers help children to grow in the Christian life when they try patiently to understand just what hinders the child. Is it a lack of understanding of what and how to do? Is it the result of too much protection, leading to an overwhelming sense of one's own value? Is the child fearful? On the answer depends the treatment.

The child in his social relationships. Much that has already been said in the discussions of the other purposes applies to the realization of this one and will not be repeated. The church should give the younger children many opportunities to show and know friendliness and good will in the community. With both older and younger children the teacher will share her own sense of responsibility for the Way of Good Will. She will lead them to participate in efforts for the welfare of their fellows and for just and fair dealings. The missionary program of the church offers many opportunities to guide children in social growth. As the children grow, their practice of kindliness and brotherhood enlarges to include many other people. Primary children are just at the age when their interests are growing beyond their own small group.

These purposes in religious guidance have been stated in terms of ways of living and of teaching. This seems wise in order to keep them practical and childlike. The other chapters of the book help teachers to see purposes carried out in ways of teaching children in the Sunday, vacation and weekday church schools, and in all other groups that the church provides for the religious guidance of Primary children.

FOR FURTHER STUDY

The following bibliography lists many more books than any one Primary teacher will ever read or be expected to read. The writer has found that one book is available to Primary teachers in one place and an equally good one in another community. For this reason it is disappointing to have a very brief list of books and never to be able to find any of them at the library. Books that are starred are for workers who wish to do advanced study in Primary work.

*Biber, Barbara, and Others. *Child Life in School.* New York: E. P. Dutton & Co., 1942. (The most careful study available.)

Bower, William Clayton. *The Living Bible.* New York: Harper & Bros., 1936. Chap. X.

*Brooks, Fowler D., and Shaffer, L. F. *Child Psychology.* Boston: Houghton Mifflin Co., 1937. Chaps. XIII-XIV. (Moral and religious development in childhood.)

Brown, Francis J. *The Sociology of Childhood.* New York: Prentice-Hall, Inc., 1939. Chap. XXIV.

*Coe, George A. *What Is Christian Education?* New York: Charles Scribner's Sons, 1920. Chaps. I, IV. (A most important discussion.)

Driscoll, Gertrude P. *How to Study the Behavior of Children.* New York: Bureau of Publications, Teachers College, Columbia University, 1941.

Education Policies Commission. *The Purposes of Education in American Democracy.* Washington: National Education Association, 1938. (Contrast your purposes with the ones set up in this study.)

Hall, Mary Ross. *Children Can See Life Whole.* New York: Association Press. 1940. Chap. I. (To help teachers learn to enter joyously and skillfully into their work. A study of how children hunt for meaning in life.)

Hockett, John A., and Jacobsen, E. W. *Modern Practices in the Elementary School.* Boston: Ginn & Co., 1938. Chaps. I, VIII-IX. (The treatment of discipline is unusually helpful.)

Hubbard, Elizabeth Vernon. *Your Children at School.* New York: John Day Co., 1942. (A creative study of the six-year-olds as they live and learn together. This is an easy book to read. It shows a profound knowledge of the six-year-olds.)

Kallen, Miriam. *The Primary Teacher Steps Out.* New York: Lothrop, Lee & Shepard Co., 1936. (To help the inexperienced teacher take the first steps in guiding active children.)

Keliher, Alice V. *Life and Growth.* New York: D. Appleton-Century Co., 1938. Part I.

*Lane, Robert H. *The Teacher in the Modern Elementary School.* Boston: Houghton Mifflin Co., 1941. Pp. 1-7; Chaps. I-II, IV. (Fine picture of elementary education today.)

*Lee, J. Murray, and Lee, Doris M. *The Child and His Curriculum.* New York: D. Appleton-Century Co., 1940. Part I. (Traces the normal growth of children as learners.)

Minor, Ruby. *Early Childhood Education.* New York: D. Appleton-Century Co., 1937. Chap. II. (This book shows how teachers may purpose and think of all their work as expressions of purposes.)

Munkres, Alberta. *Which Way for Our Children?* New York: Charles Scribner's Sons, 1936. Chaps. I-II.

*Saucier, W. A. *Theory and Practice in the Elementary School.* New York: The Macmillan Co., 1941. Chaps. I, IV.

Sherrill, Lewis J. *The Opening Doors of Childhood.* New York: The Macmillan Co., 1939. Chap. I.

———*Understanding Children.* New York: Abingdon-Cokesbury Press, 1939.

*Skinner, Charles E., and Harriman, Philip L. *Child Psychology.* New York: The Macmillan Co., 1941. Chap. XII. (A careful study of some problems and approaches in the religious teaching of children. A provocative study of religious growth.)

Smither, Ethel L. *Understanding Our Purposes.* Nashville: The Methodist Publishing House, 1941. (Free pamphlet.)

———*The Use of the Bible with Children.* New York: Abingdon-Cokesbury Press, 1937. Chaps. I-III, VII.

Stott, Leila V. *Eight Year Old Merchants.* New York: Greenberg, Publisher, Inc., 1928. (A picture of active learning of eight-year-olds. An older book but easy to read. Shows how able eight-year-olds are.)

*Tiegs, Ernest W. *The Management of Learning in the Elementary Schools,* New York: Longmans, Green & Co., 1937. Chap. I.

Washburne, Carleton W. *A Living Philosophy of Education.* New York: John Day Co., 1940. Introduction; Chaps. III, IX. (An important book for any teacher.)

38 PRIMARY CHILDREN

FOR FURTHER ACTIVITY

1. Start a card file to record what you learn about the children in your group. Use a large card. Of course, the record will be a confidential one. Consult the public-school teacher to learn more about the child. You may wish at first to observe one or two children at a session. Date each observation. What do they do and say? Are they silent most of the time? What do you know about the child's home life? What is his position in the family? Is he an only child, eldest, youngest, middle? Is he an adopted child?

Try to keep an objective record. That is, avoid expressing judgment on what you observe. Instead of saying, "Jack is such a friendly child. He shared his crayons with Tom," record, "Jack shared his crayons with Tom today. The boys came to church together." Make records at regular intervals.

2. If a mother entered a child in your group for the first time and asked what your purposes for the children were, what would you answer? Write a statement of purpose in 750 words.

3. Suppose a father brought two children to your group, one six years old, the other eight. "I want them kept together because they are brother and sister," he says. How would you explain to him their differing abilities and religious needs?

4. A member of the official board of your church wishes to know why Primary children cannot attend adult assemblies regularly with profit. What would you tell him?

5. List at least ten questions of children that reveal religious needs. How has this study of child need and teacher purpose influenced your thinking about these questions?

6. A boy who already has a reputation for badness enters the Primary group. You are assured by a number of adults that you had better discourage his attendance because he cannot be helped. How would you proceed to guide him?

Chapter II

HELPING PRIMARY CHILDREN TO LEARN

HELPING Primary children to learn in the field of religion means that the Primary teachers must know how children learn in other phases of their experience. After an understanding is gained of how learning takes place, the church-school teacher will use this knowledge to determine her use of method and material and to evaluate her plans.

Human learning is a complex process. Sometimes insight comes as quickly as a lightning flash. Sometimes knowledge grows as gradually as the dawn in a northern land. No one can say just when mastery is established. Sometimes a person learns so unconsciously that he thinks he inherited the attitude, fear, or attachment. Primary children learn in all these ways. To see a Primary child's face grow radiant with a sudden insight is to look on true loveliness. Most of the learnings of Primary children, however, are gained in more gradual fashion. Many of the learnings that influence his emotional behavior are largely unconscious ones. In the field of values, and of religion, experience is gradually bringing understanding. Ideas of God are not yet clearly organized, but foundations for them are being surely laid. A knowledge of the religious heritage, as of the Bible, is necessarily limited and unfixed.

This is a period of life when the teacher may work for foundations of religious ideas, for the beginnings of standards of conduct that are the expressions of a Christian viewpoint, and for healthy emotional attitudes that influence religious development. She will expect the children to be slow in gaining sharply defined religious ideas. If the teacher understands the theories of how children learn, she will have a better grasp on how to nurture religious growth during the Primary years.

Learning comes through insight. One theory of how learning occurs is called learning through seeing patterns, or insight into relationships. A most practical description of learning by insight was given by a mother one day: "It's like coming out of a fog, isn't it? One day your understanding is hazy. You fumble around. Then you see things fit together and belong that way." Learning goes on when the child puts together parts of his environment that have hitherto seemed to have no connection. Or he learns meaning and relationships because of his experiences with people.

At first a child's understandings are vague. He thinks only in terms of objects and places that he can see and touch, feel, smell, and taste. In other words, he is literal-minded and is limited in imagination to what he has experienced through his senses. A six-year-old at the zoo exclaimed: "O, Mother, look at the little spotted dogs!" He was watching some fallow deer from India. He thought all four-footed animals with the general appearance of dogs were dogs. As he grows, of course, he will learn to distinguish among many species of small animals and will know many kinds in each species. At present he lumps them all together. Children often struggle to understand the meaning of words. "What is short?" a seven-year-old asked. She understood when two children, one tall and one short, stood side by side.

Young Primary children understand human relationships in vague fashion also. Even the older ones are struggling with them. "Is a brother a boy?" asked a brilliant seven-year-old. She had no brothers, or the word would have had greater meaning. Taking large, vague ideas and filling in their details is one way that children learn. Starting with many small ideas and gradually classifying them under a large one is a second way that insight comes. An adult can realize how learning means putting ideas and knowledge into patterns if he will recall the time when he first moved to a strange city. He learned first to know the locations that were most necessary to him, but he learned each one separately. He could go from home to place of business. From there he knew how to get to the bank or the shopping center or the club. However, he did not know how to take short cuts from one of these places to another. Then the day came when all these now familiar places fitted into a map of the town. He knew his way around at last.

Children learn to live the Christian life in their daily relationships in this same way. They master, bit by bit, Christian ideas, and finally classify what they learn to make a generalized idea or habit or way of feeling. They learn to practice and understand honesty, kindliness, gentleness, dependability, just as the man learned to know his city. For example, the child learns to be honest in many practical situations. He does not classify these ways of behaving as honesty at first. Each one stands by itself in his thinking. Each one is a separate insight. Then in older childhood the boys and girls begin to build a general idea of honesty by classifying all of these ways of acting under the one name. The more vivid and the more practical the experiences the child has had, the clearer his insight into the way of acting will be. The less he is confused and hurried into thinking about it in general terms or large patterns, the richer the idea will be and the more influence it will have on his daily living. Primary teachers who make talks to children about honesty, obedience, loyalty, trust, and so on, are likely to confuse them. They are putting the cart before the horse, so to speak. They are using a highly abstract word before the children have enough experience in living to profit by talking about it. The Primary teacher who really helps her children live in Christian ways puts living first. She expects insight to grow from experience. She gives additional experience to correct wrong insights based on misunderstanding.

Three boys in a class of eight-year-olds plagued a substitute teacher unmercifully. When their regular church-school teacher returned, she decided this was a problem that must not be ignored. The other children were excited by what had happened, even though they did not approve of the boys' lack of courtesy and friendliness toward a person who was trying to help them. The group decided how to help the boys remember in the future. The boys were to see the substitute and show her in practical ways how sorry they were for failing to be friendly. It was a solemn moment.

"Oh, my!" said Tom with a sigh. "Now I know what being 'dependable' means."

"You have some new ideas about it," the teacher said. "The whole class does. And we'll keep right on finding out more about it."

These children had a big, vague insight that experience was enriching.

The following quotation shows how children learn ways of behaving and gain insight into the Christian meaning of life. Sometimes parents and teachers take for granted that children know what they can only l rn slowly and under patient guidance. They have forgott.. how life required the same thing of them.

In a child's life much is experiment that for an adult is no longer experimental at all. We have not half appreciated the extent to which, if the mind is to develop to its full capacity, childhood and youth must abound in experimental approaches. I have in my possession a photograph of a baby that is having his first experience of crawling upon a lawn. In the whole bodily attitude, and especially in the look upon the face, one beholds the young explorer. No arctic hero about to reach the Pole could express more of this spirit. Let this be a symbol of personality engaged in finding itself. We can no more solve our pupils' problems for them than we could carry this baby to his destination. The art in Christian education must consist in inducing pupils to make experiments that, being real at the stage of the learner's experience, will show where the truth lies, and at the same time leave the personality fresh for further experimentation.[1]

It is a great help to the teacher to understand how gradually children learn, how slowly they master the Christian idea of God and philosophy of life. She does not grow dis-

[1] George A. Coe, *What Is Christian Education?* Charles Scribner's Sons, 1925, p. 289.

couraged because the class seems to be standing still, nor does she expect suddenly to accomplish unusual growth. The teacher welcomes problems and questions instead of being disturbed by them. She regards them as chances to teach, not as interruptions of her plans. She expects to do the same thing over and over that understanding may come.

One class had a reputation for fighting. The teacher held group and private conferences with the children. She introduced many different, interesting plans which required friendly co-operation for success. She set an example of good humor and often showed how there were much better ways of solving difficulties than fighting. The group learned of people who practiced these ways. The teacher showed how friends of Jesus were known for their friendliness and gentleness. His kindliness was referred to. The children were led in prayers that expressed what they themselves had said about wanting strength to work out difficulties in more friendly ways. One day this teacher said to a friend: "I have been checking and, so far as I can discover, there has not been a fight for three months. I hope that they will continue to be infrequent." She had been working in church school, in vacation church school, and with the homes for nearly fourteen months. Surely "If we faint not" applies to the teacher of young children in the church. Learning through insights may seem to come quickly, but this long process of living is the basis for much of this learning.

Learnings grow through associations. Children often learn unconsciously, especially in the field of emotions. They are conditioned in certain ways because of connections that grow up between quite unrelated events, persons, or places. The emotion or attitude to the first transfers to the other. This is unreasoned learning. It is powerful in its effect upon a person because it occurs so often in early childhood and goes on either unconsciously or is forgotten. It is a kind of learning that has tremendous importance in religious growth.

A great many fears, superstitions, prejudices, and resentments start in this way. They are learned, not inherited.

For example, a little child is playing alone in the garden. He is feeling cross this morning because he did not sleep well the night before. Without warning, an awkward collie puppy bounds upon the baby, knocks him over, and chews on his hand roughly enough to hurt. The child responds to pain much more easily because he is already tired and upset. The puppy's sudden attack makes him want to run away. He cannot get up fast enough, so he screams. His mother runs to him. She calls out in an anxious voice. Her actions make his fear seem much more important to the child. The next time the child sees a dog, he runs and screams with fear. He even dislikes to play under the shady tree where he first met the collie puppy.

The days and years slip by. Jack is a Primary child. Both the mother and the boy have forgotten about the morning long ago. The mother tells his teacher: "Jack is a strange child. He is so afraid of dogs. I think he inherited it from my mother. She never could stand a dog near her." Jack was born with no fear of any kind. But he had the ability to respond with feeling to what happened to him. He learned his fear of dogs and of playing under trees, which his mother also mentions, from life.

This type of learning is at the bottom of many of the behavior problems of children and of adults. "I just don't like ———(another racial group). I was born that way." Prejudices like fears are learned, not inherited. Many of our likes and dislikes, our friendships and our enmities grow out of experiences like that of the baby with the dog. We transfer our dislike of a person with whom we have had an early disagreeable experience to all persons who are in any way like him. After a prejudice or a fear starts, people close their minds to facts that might lead to different ideas about the object of fear or prejudice. Only facts that back up the attitude make an impression. To know that this kind of learning is going on in every life is truly a weapon in the hands of the mature Christian who wishes to overcome his fears and prej-

udices and to help children to meet theirs constructively. Many
a fear that hinders the growth of fellowship with God starts
in just this way. It is better to avoid them if we can; for,
while unlearning them is possible, it is difficult.

Teachers and parents can also help children to learn positive likes and attitudes by being careful of the associations
they build up. Think of the church experience. A child should
associate the church with pleasant, friendly people—ones who
are steady and dependable. He should think of it as a place
where he can think as a child, act as a child, and be as secure
as a child needs to be. He should feel that at church he will
have his problems understood. He should experience friendliness, wonder, joy, good will, a sense of at-homeness and of
the reality of God.

One wonders what associations a child has with the church
when he is hurried on Sunday through a hasty breakfast by
sleepy adults, arrives late, is crowded into a not-too-clean
room, sits still to listen to an adult whom he does not know
very well. He may never see his teacher except briefly on
Sunday. Much that she says is confusing to him. Contrast
with this child's experience that of the boy or girl who lives
in a home where Sunday and churchgoing are anticipated and
planned for. There is no rush on Sunday morning. He arrives
at church to meet teachers who are his friends and who receive him in a place that is attractive and childlike. He has
many chances to learn. His teachers are growing steadily in
teaching skill, in the depth of their religious experience, and
in their knowledge of child life. One need not ask in which
case association with the church is likely to lay foundations of
interest, loyalty, and sacrifice. Primary teachers and other
church members should feel challenged to make the latter kind
of primary experience a reality in their church and not regard
it as an ideal that might be reached under perfect conditions. It is encouraging to know that many parents and teachers in average churches are providing such an environment
for their children on Sunday.

Children learn through activity. Children learn when
they actively investigate their environment, use materials to

carry out thoughtful purposes, experiment with them, and solve problems that are genuine ones to them. They learn also through varied chances to use eyes, ears, nose, hands, and mouth. The church school cannot afford to rely only on seeing and hearing, sometimes just on hearing. Teaching is vague unless it gives a child chances to use his senses. Children can look at objects, feel them, use them in play. They can come close to another group when they eat some of the food that is common to that country and people. They can get a sense of reality about Bible lands in the same way. They can learn to feel akin to the people of the Bible or to members of some national church when they take part in some of their occupations. When they were finding out about Palestinian life, one third grade ground barley between stones. "Isn't it hard work?" they said. "Yet they always thanked God for the food," the teacher said. "After they worked so hard?" one little girl asked in wonder.

Children can learn to accept responsibility for other people and so to practice Christian brotherhood. One group made apple jelly in the church kitchen on Saturday. They were going to give it as a Thanksgiving present to a home for old ladies. Mothers helped. Church work spills over into the week when it is genuine living for children. The children smelled the apple juice boiling, the sugar heating. They saw the clear, red of the jelly. It tasted good on crackers. They helped to seal the jars and to wrap them in orange cellophane. The presents looked lovely when they were ready. "We could sing for them," the children said. So they learned a song of praise. They worshiped through the song. The children were learning, through all sorts of sensory experiences, to serve others. Vivid teaching is the kind that is never forgotten by a child. Sensory appeals help to make teaching vivid.

Then there are the three boys who attended a church where they were enrolled in a younger Primary group, six-and-seven-year-olds. The session was a brief one, but it was carefully planned to give the children the kinds of experiences that lead to learning. As Easter time approached, two of the boys came to their teacher with a grape box they had found in the supply closet.

"This would make a good cart to put our eggs in," Roger announced.

"Yes," said the leader, "but we'd need wheels."

"I'll bring some off an old wagon of mine," said Milton.

"My daddy will put it together," said Buddy.

"We'll paint it green," said Roger.

"Wait a minute," said the leader, sensing that this was an ambitious bit of work. "It will mean a lot of work and . . ."

"We'll do it," said Roger firmly. "Will you bring the paint?"

"Yes," said the leader, "if you are sure your mothers won't mind. Will you bring smocks? I'll bring along some turpentine."

"We'll ask them." Away they went to the adult class. They came back shortly with the mothers' permissions and promises of the smocks.

Buddy's daddy put wheels and box together and used the handle of an old broom to make the tongue. The boys sandpapered, painted, repainted. Their cart was done, ready for the Easter eggs they were sending to a church center. "Well," said Buddy, his father all over again, "we've made it, fellows, with Miss ——— doing a dab here and there!" The three stood off and viewed their work with joy and pride.

A third grade planned to send a Negro child to a summer camp. Their money was locked in a cupboard where their own treasurer placed it. During the week a petty thief broke into the church and took the box with the children's money. On Sunday the children were so excited that they could not settle down. Their threats against the robber were dire. The leader let them "work off steam" for a time.

"What will ——— [the Negro child] do now?" she asked quietly. There was dead silence.

"Our money is gone," said Russell.

"It will be pleasant out at the camp this summer," added their teacher. "The little child for whom you were saving has never seen a stream. Hurting the robber won't send him to camp."

"Maybe," said Barbara slowly, "we could start again." She put five cents on the table. The idea "caught on." The children saved the money again, and the child had his vacation. They had learned how to face defeat in a constructive fashion and how to persevere in good will. They looked at a wrong done to them from another's point of view. They learned "to build again," as each worker in the Kingdom must if he is to press on to the goal of his high calling.

Purposeful living and learning. The children in the Primary groups that have just been described experienced an active, eager, thoughtful church life in which they could be themselves, face real problems, and have guidance in solving them. While all the purposes of Primary group life in the church cannot be shared with children, it is surprising how the group may have its own understanding of what is worth while.

Once a photographer asked permission to take pictures of the significant activities of a certain group. "I wonder what they are," the leader asked herself. The Primary workers picked out fifteen as meaningful ones. "Let's ask the children," the leader suggested. So the next Sunday she said, "Mr. ———— wishes to take pictures of us to show other Primary children and their teachers how we live and work together here at church. I decided to ask you what you would choose as the important things that we do."

Out of the fifteen types of activity chosen by the leaders, the children selected thirteen. They were: having a conference, caring for the room, making a gift for their mothers (clay bowls for pansies), making a frieze to record awakening life in springtime, sharing stories and books in the reading corner, giving the minister the first flower from their bulb garden to wear when he preached, looking at a flower through a magnifying glass to see its design, singing, playing a game. Why should not Primary children see purpose back of their activities, provided the work and plans are thoroughly suited to their needs and abilities?

The Primary class is a mass of pent-up energy crying out for guidance. Teaching should release it for good. One teacher received the suggestion that she make her children responsible for the care of their room. "They wouldn't know how," was her first thought. "They never notice how the room is arranged," was the second one. Then she decided to give the children a chance. The class was working on a unit, "Learning to Help at Church." The boys and girls suddenly came alive. They were full of ideas. They consulted the Primary superintendent about a new arrangement. With her consent, the class went to work. "My, I'm glad that piano is moved," said one of the boys. "I never liked the way it kept us from seeing Mrs. ———— [the superintendent]." The teacher discovered that the children had been waiting for an opportunity to take part in the care of the room and that their pride in it grew in proportion to their responsibility.

Learning fostered by variety of plan. The Primary class and department help children to learn, also, when their individual differences and varying maturities are cared for. Once a Primary group decided to find the friendly people in their community who were working with God. Over in one corner one interested group built a friendly town.[2] It turned out to be their own neighborhood square. It was a thoroughly childlike way of recording what the children were learning about working with God in their own community. It was connected with all their plans for the year. A second group made riddles about these friendly people and planned to visit them.[3] A third group placed pictures of helpers on a screen.[4] A picture of Jesus was included. The entire group enjoyed stories about how he brought more abundant life to any place that he entered. In another part of the room a group painted a mural of helpers.[5] Some children listened to a good reader who had found one or two of Rachel Field's poems about helpers.[6] At the piano a group learned to sing a song about

[2] Any first grade might use this plan.
[3] A second-grade plan.
[4] A third-grade pla·
[5] A second-grade plan.
[6] A third-grade plan.

people who showed friendliness. The environment of that Primary group was rich enough to let each child learn through activities that were most suited to him.

Checking on learning. Children not only need experiences but should learn to think about what they have done, heard, and seen. Of course, they will not be hurried into such expressions. But unless the leader checks on how and what they are thinking, Primary children are likely to gain confused and incorrect ideas from even suitable activities. A second grade visited the sanctuary of their church one Sunday. It was like a beautiful thirteenth-century Gothic chapel. Among other lovely elements, there was an ever-burning light that hung suspended before the altar. The electric wire that carried current to it was almost invisible. The children had gone up into the gallery to sit quietly and to enjoy the lovely light, the sound of the organ, the beautiful white stone columns, the red of the cushions in the pews. They sat quietly for a time. "I see it," said Joe, eyes shining. "I do, too," came from here and there in the group. They were on a level with the light. "It's magic," whispered Jerry. "Yes, it's magic," one child after another repeated. Now magic means magician's tricks to a Primary child. "No," said the leader firmly, "it is a lovely light. There is no need to think that it is magic. There is a very small wire that carries electricity to it. That is why it gives light. Ask Harry [the sexton] about it when you get a chance. I think the light in our church is beautiful enough without being magic." The group sat quietly to look at the beautiful reredos with the light before it. They were learning to separate magic from wonder and worship because the teacher had helped them to approach an experience thoughtfully. She knew how easy it is for superstitions to grow up in connection with religion and that many of them become fixed during the Primary years.[7] The foundations of an understanding of God as spirit and of a religion that is spiritual are laid most surely by careful teaching during these years of change from younger to older childhood.

[7] See Piaget, *Child's Conception of the World.* Harcourt, Brace & Co., 1929.

Older Primary children also need help in thinking in religious areas.

"Did Jesus make magic?" asked Albert.

"I think he did," said Tom, his best friend.

"When Jesus chose how he would work and explained what he was going to do," the teacher said, "he chose not to do magic things that would just make people follow after him and be surprised at what he did."

"And he didn't want to do magic?" insisted Albert.

"No," the teacher answered, "he said that it would be a wrong use of the power that God had given him."

"Well," said Tom.

The brief exclamation told the teacher much. She knew that the boy had gained a new insight into the teachings and purposes of Jesus and that he should now be left to work with it.[8]

The children in both of these incidents were not pressed to think beyond the level of their maturities. In the first case, the teacher made no attempt to explain the symbolism of light in a Christian church. In the second example, the teacher did not attempt to introduce an explanation of miracles. Children learn to think well and to be interested in finding answers to religious problems when they have teachers who stimulate them to think, know how far they can go in their thinking, and give them only so much guidance as they need.

Learning new meaning in the familiar. With the younger Primary children especially, learning goes on best when it is kept in familiar areas. The child at six and seven is familiar with his immediate world in a more superficial way than we sometimes realize. He needs chances to see new meanings in everyday things, to build up more religious understanding of the life around him instead of being hurried off into the long ago and the far away. He needs many chances to practice friendliness and good will. Chances to gain religious meaning in experiences with na-

---

[8] Readers will see that the leader was interpreting the third and fourth chapters of Luke in this incident.

ture may be planned. New experiences in family relationships are initiated in a well-planned church program but
go back into the home to make life there more satisfying
and beautiful. Additional opportunities to have friendly relations with other children and with people in the church
and community are provided. These are the important opportunities through which young Primary children grow
religiously.

Learning comes through new points of view. Older
Primary children gain social and religious understanding
of their world as they contrast their ways of living with
those of another race or place, or study some phase of the
other group's life against the background of their own ways
of living. Often children gain new insights and see new meanings through companionship with fine adults in the church or
the community. They learn to see from the point of view of
the new friends. This is especially valuable experience for the
third grade, who must have contact with new points of view
and new understandings of cause and effect in human affairs
or they grow narrow, self-satisfied, and patronizing.

Learning and individual need. Learning takes place in
a Primary group when the children are free to move around
in an orderly way, to investigate, to use materials, and to
face problems, which they are expected to solve thoughtfully.
The children who are passive, quiet, unresponsive, who are
"good and never give any trouble" are the ones for whom
the leader should be anxious.[9] There may be some fear, timid-
ity, or emotional tension that the teacher must help the child
overcome before he can learn. A child may cease to grow at
church because he feels like a stranger.

Clifford came Sunday after Sunday, sat in a chair in his
group, worked without real interest, answered in monosyl-
lables. He was in, not of, the group. Then Christmas Sunday
came. The leaders, pianist, and children sang their best-loved
Christmas songs. Suddenly Clifford spoke directly to the
pianist: "Do you know 'Jingle Bells'?"

[9] See E. K. Wickham, *Children's Behavior and Teacher's Judgment*, Common-
wealth Fund Division of Publications, N. Y., 1929.

"Why, yes."

"Play it for me."

She began, and Clifford started to sing. Other children joined in with Clifford leading them. It was a glorious time, although the leader never would have used this song at church.

"How did you like it?" Clifford asked the leader. "Fine. It was so jolly," she said.

Clifford was one of the group from that time on. He was a very bright child and a leader. Often bright children take time to adjust because they sense the situation more keenly and hold aloof until they are sure of themselves and have confidence in the teacher.

The teacher's place. In every one of the cases of learning that have been reported the teacher was a most important factor. What kind of teachers help Primary children to learn religiously?

First of all, the leader should be a deeply spiritual person with a genuine religious experience; for the young child learns as much from what the adult is as from what she says. Her trust in God and the presence of the living Christ in her life color all her influence.

She should be a person who has solved her own emotional conflicts to a reasonable degree. The Primary teacher should be happy in her own social relationships. Unless she has real poise, no assumption of a calm manner will set a group at ease; for the children plumb to the depths of personality and find confusion or security there.

The Primary teacher should be able to work well with other adults, for children learn to love their fellows when they have the guidance of leaders who are trying to live in love and charity with their neighbors.

The Primary teacher should be a good Bible student. Only the adult who really knows the Bible and the child will know what parts of the Bible to share with children and how and when to share them.

The Primary teacher should be a person who finds joy and renewal from being with children. To be one of a group of Primary teachers who are joyful because of some wonderful insight, or response, or purpose of their children is to know the glory of life. Not only must teachers understand children, but, to be good Primary teachers, they must have a certain childlike quality that makes a common bond with them. To keep one's childlikeness is to remain capable of growth, of trust, of joy in religion.

The Primary teacher should be growing as a teacher. When she uses a method, she does it well. When she helps her class to plan and carry out an activity, she shows skill. She has a pride in good workmanship that keeps her studying and learning. This quality wins the children's respect for the church.

What are some of the teacher's responsibilities? She provides the environment in which the children can learn. This includes the emotional and social atmosphere of the group as well as a good place to work and adequate materials to work with.

She helps a child to purpose and plan and to see new meaning in old experience. She also broadens his understanding and helps him gain a more Christian point of view. She introduces him to broader experiences, new social opportunities, new chances to wonder and to search for meaning. She is both a stimulator and a guide.

She is the child's source of security at church school. His trust in her, in her friendly understanding, her sense of fun, her dependability, is his foundation for living bravely and helpfully, especially when he is six years old.

The teacher is a religious guide. She seeks to help the child find a better way of living just as the physician helps him to find a healthier one.

She is the children's consultant when they have problems of an emotional nature or curiosities that they wish to satisfy. She helps them to find out or to plan. She helps them to find relief from too heavy pressures of life. She shares their joys and triumphs, goes to their musical programs and their parents' nights at school. She rejoices over the new baby, is steady and present in times of trouble. She is a fortunate person, a learner as well as the steady friend of Primary children.

FOR FURTHER STUDY

Choose the ones that are available and that meet your needs. Those starred are for advanced study.

Baxter, Bernice. *Teacher-Pupil Relationships.* New York: The Macmillan Co., 1941.

*Bode, Boyd H. *How We Learn.* Boston: D. C. Heath & Co., 1940. Chaps. I, XI, XVI.

*Chave, Ernest J. *Personality Development in Children.* Chicago: University of Chicago Press, 1937.

*Coe, George A. *A Social Theory of Religious Education.* New York: Charles Scribner's Sons, 1917. Chap. XI.

*Hartshorne, Hugh. *Character in Human Relations.* New York: Charles Scribner's Sons, 1933. Chaps. XXI-XXIV.

*Henry, Nelson B., editor. *The Psychology of Learning.* Forty-first Yearbook of the National Society for the Study of Education, Part II. Bloomington, Ill.: Public School Publishing Co., 1942.

Hockett, John A., and Jacobsen, E. W. *Modern Practices in the Elementary School.* Boston: Ginn & Co., 1938. Chaps. II, VIII.

Lee, J. Murray, and Lee, Doris M. *The Child and His Curriculum.* New York: D. Appleton-Century Co., 1940. Chap. V.

McLester, Frances Cole. *Achieving Christian Character.* Nashville: Abingdon-Cokesbury Press, 1937.

Minor, Ruby. *Early Childhood Education.* New York: D. Appleton-Century Co., 1937. Chap. VI.

Myers, A. J. W. *What Is Religious Education?* London: National Sunday School Union.

*Reed, Homer B. *Psychology of Elementary School Subjects.* Boston: Ginn & Co., 1938. Chap. III.

*Saucier, W. A. *Theory and Practice in the Elementary School.* New York: The Macmillan Co., 1941. Chap. II.

*Shaffer, Laurance F. *The Psychology of Adjustment.* Boston: Houghton Mifflin Co., 1936. Chap. III, Parts III, IV. (Very technical but important.)

Smith, Robert S. *New Trails for the Christian Teacher.* Philadelphia: Presbyterian Board of Christian Education, 1934.

Tiegs, Ernest W. *The Management of Learning in the Elementary Schools.* New York: Longmans, Green & Co., 1937. Chap. II.

Witty, Paul A. and Skinner, Charles E. *Mental Hygiene in Modern Education.* New York: Farrar & Rinehart, Inc., 1939. Chaps. II, VI.

Zyve, Claire T., compiler. *Growth Through School Living.* Washington Association for Childhood Education, 1940.

FOR FURTHER ACTIVITY

1. Try to find out just what your children think about the words **(1)** home, **(2)** church, **(3)** parents, **(4)** family, **(5)** good, **(6)** bad, **(7)** kind, **(8)** happy. Then try to find out what they think of when they hear the word God. Ask them such questions as "What is a home?" "What is a church?" "What does the word good mean?" (A third-grade question.) Ask the first grade, "When are you good?" Ask the questions of individuals, not of a group. As soon as possible write down what the children say.

2. Summarize what their answers reveal about the insights of primary children.

3. Give an example of how you have learned by suddenly gaining insight.

4. Give an example, if you can, of some learning by association.

5. Give an example of how you learned through some social experience; through some sensory experience.

6. Tell of how some religious truth took on greater meaning because of your purposeful living.

7. List ten ways that you have attempted to teach during the last month through sensory experience, that ˙ through sight hearing, smell, taste, touch.

8. Describe the adult who most influenced you before you were nine years old. Was he a member of your family, a teacher ⁀ teacher at church?

9. Study one unit in the course of study you are now teaching. Make a list of its purposes. Then in a parallel column list the activities that are used to achieve them. Allow for at least three other columns, a. you will need this paper later on.

10. What prejudices hinder you in your Christian experience How did they arise? Can you plan ways to outgrow them?

Chapter III

USING ENVIRONMENT AND CURRICULUM TO GUIDE PRIMARY CHILDREN

EVERY experience that the church gives its Primary children, either deliberately or unconsciously, is a part of the curriculum for their religious guidance. All of the Primary child's meaningful contacts with other persons at church help or hinder his religious growth. Experiences that come from the use of the printed course of study add another part of the curriculum of a Primary department. Leaders may study first the room or rooms that the church provides for the Primary children. Then the printed course of study and its contribution may be examined. Chapter VIII will discuss the effect of the fellowship in the church on the religious growth of the children.

A place to live and grow. Rooms speak to children in a clear voice. It would be an interesting plan for the Primary leaders to sit down some day and attune their ears to the message of the room in which they teach.

Some rooms are bright and shining. Conscientious leaders arrange them in such perfect order, and place such beautiful objects in them, that they say to children: "Look around, but don't disturb. This is a place that your teachers have prepared for you." Some rooms say by their dusty, disorderly condition and by the piles of worn-out furniture pushed into the corners: "The people of this church do not consider the religious teaching of children important enough to provide a proper place for them. Nor do the people of this church love the building enough to keep it clean." Some rooms—they may be the simplest ones—say: "This place of beauty is for children. This room is for you to use, to care for, and to enjoy. It belongs to you."

57

How does a room speak to young children? Through cleanliness, beauty, good arrangement to serve its purpose, and by the chances that it gives them to be active. A room should be so arranged that the children begin to work or investigate or sing on arrival. There should be every evidence of ongoing life. Work begun previously should be where the children can begin on it at once. Some rooms are so arranged that they appeal to many different interests.

Here is a reading table with attractive books and pictures. It is in a quiet corner by a window. Or there may be, instead—as I once saw in a small, two-room church in Wisconsin—an attractive bookcase made by the children themselves out of an orange crate, with a stool placed invitingly near it. Or again, as in one tiny rural church in Virginia, there may be books invitingly placed on a window ledge with a low bench under it. The book table or corner or ledge says: "Come. You are learning to read. Look at the pictures and read. Find answers to your own questions. These books were chosen for you to study and to enjoy." [1]

One sees also a table of objects. The third grade gather about it. They handle each article. Questions come thick and fast. A new experience in understanding has been launched because a table or case of objects has said: "There are many people on this earth, our home. Some live as you do, and some very differently. They are all children of God, our Father. Come, learn to know them." Then sympathies are widened and brotherly interests stimulated. Space is not necessary for the teacher to see that children have such helps to learning. One resourceful teacher carries a basket of books, objects, and work materials to and fro in her car. They make her corner of a small rural church a real place of learning for her Primary class.

Here is a case or cupboard of neatly labeled materials that children may use in working out ideas and expressing what they think and feel. There are clay, paper, blueprint paper, paints, crayons, wood, and simple tools. There is a

[1] See lists of books for Primary children at end of Chap. V.

large box of materials that have been collected here and there by teachers and children. This supply case says: "Arrange supplies on a table each Sunday so that each class or group may find what they need. Select what you can use to express your ideas and carry out your plans. What can you add to these supplies?"

Now the teachers look at the piano. A friendly pianist is ready to play for the children. Some chairs stand near the instrument. There are attractive songbooks. One contains illustrated copies of songs compiled from the children's folders. It was made by a third grade. "I love music, don't you?" says this arrangement. "Come, let us sing unto the Lord."

Under a window that looks out on a lawn stands a low table. It holds a square container for gold fish. Several bowls of bulbs are sending out strong, green leaves. A turtle lives in a shallow bowl. A watering can stands on one corner of the table. At one side of the window hangs a chart. It is written in manuscript writing.[2] It says: "Have you looked at our garden? Something happened there this week." This part of the room says: "Living, growing things make me wonder. Sunshine and water make them grow, but we have a part also. What do you wonder about when you work in our outdoor garden?"

Here is a bulletin board. It is a large piece of beaverboard set in a wooden frame. It might be a sheet of Manila or wrapping paper attached to a screen or the wall, or hung from a window sill. The children run to read it when they come. The superintendent posts their work on it after she has consulted with the teachers. Here children and teachers place records of what each class is doing. There are reports of public school and home plans. The children rejoice with each other over good news.

There is also a part of the room that is kept for conference, and for more formal worship times than the moments

---

[2] This writing is used with Primary children in many public schools. See Edith U. Conard, *Trends in Manuscript Writing*, Teachers College, Columbia University, 1936.

of worship that may occur in any part of the room and at any time. The entire department comes here for quietness, and for thought about purposes, successes, and failures. It is a place of beauty with one or two lovely pictures. Flowers, berries, and grasses in season add to its attractiveness. Treasures brought by teachers, children, or adult friends are found here. Sometimes a record of work is placed in this part of the room. This is also a place for fellowship. The children should feel responsible for caring for it. They may work by groups or take turns by classes. The arrangement should be simple and childlike. The writer avoids the use of candles, except at Christmas, as lending an unnatural effect to a room for young children.

In another part of the room there are tables for work. They invite children to be active, not to sit and listen. Of course, at times Primary children like to work on the floor if the piece of work—as, for instance, a mural—is a large one. So the room is organized to carry out the purposes that were set up in Chapter I and to supply the conditions for learning that were discussed in Chapter II.

The Primary course of study. Now the Primary course of study may be discussed. A printed course of study helps teachers in several ways that are so important that even experienced teachers use one. Let us see what these ways are.

First, the course of study makes sure that there is balance, or well-rounded experience, for the children. Great care goes into its development so that all the major purposes of religious guidance [3] receive the proper emphasis at each age level. It protects a child from a narrow or dull experience at church by providing proper sequence; that is, the experiences follow each other in a normal way. The proper amount of time and emphasis is given to each purpose.

A course of study makes available a rich body of source material. It includes varied suggestions of plans and methods. Busy teachers welcome its provision of songs, selected poems, Bible verses, and stories.

[3] See pp. 28-36.

The course of study can help the teacher to grow in skill as a leader of children. She can compare her own methods with the ones that are included in the course and learn how to improve her ways of teaching.

A good course of study represents the combined judgment of a number of experienced Primary workers regarding religious needs and how to meet them. If it is carelessly or slavishly followed, it is ineffective. If one course is used in the Primary Department and a course from another series in the Junior, chaos is the result. Discriminatingly used, a course of study is stimulating and helpful to the teacher.

The unit of work or of guided experience. Most Primary courses of study are now organized around certain problems, groups of experiences, and needs of children. This organization is entitled a "unit" of work, or of guided experience. Some teachers call thoroughly childlike units "centers of interest." There are many names given at present to these units into which a course of study is organized. Some people use a name to mean one kind of unit, and the same name is used by others with a different meaning. The writer prefers the term "unit of guided experience" to "unit of work"; for so many people have used the latter to describe a study unit, not a work unit at all. In a "unit of guided experience" child problem, purpose, activity, and thought should be central. Materials are chosen to help along the living of the group. Some units of work start at the other end. They choose units of subject matter to teach and then add problems and so on to them. The study unit of this type may be questioned as too mature an approach to learning for Primary children.

In a way, a unit of guided experience is like a story. It has a beginning that arouses or utilizes and centers interests in certain purposes, activities, and desires to learn. These initiating or beginning steps may take one or several class periods. Then the unit moves by a series of successive steps that are cumulative in effect; that is, they build upon one another to a climax. These are developmental sessions and usually take a number of class periods. This climax may mean the carrying out of the purpose, the solution of the problem, or the discovery of the desired knowledge. Often it includes all three. Then there is the end, where the group feel that they have, with satisfaction, solved their problem or reached their goal. They may share their achievements with parents or friends. These are judging or evaluating sessions and require about two class periods.

A unit also follows the steps in an act of thinking. First, the group faces a difficulty or feels a curiosity or a desire to know and to do. Second, the children make purposes to solve these problems. Third, they plan how to do so. Fourth, they carry out these plans. And fifth, the group evaluates its own successes and failures. Of course, these steps are not strung out like beads on a string. They are more like the warp and woof of a cloth; purposing, planning, executing, judging—each step fulfills and stimulates the others. They weave back and forth as new purposes arise and plans are made.

Place of teaching materials. Teaching materials—like songs, poems, Bible verses, stories, pictures—help the group to solve their own problems and carry out their own purposes. They enrich the living of the group. They are not an end in themselves. In other words, the teacher tells a story or teaches a hymn or a Bible verse when this material guides the children to act, think, and feel in more religious fashion. The activities of class and department are the real "lessons," for they make it possible to accomplish purposes. The activities provide for the living and discovery and also include ways of expressing and recording what the group is learning.

Units of experience. The plan for one session leads from and into another. There is no such thing as a single lesson that stands all by itself. If a thoroughly important experience so enriches a unit that more time is needed than has been indicated in the written plans, some other unit should be dropped from the year's work to allow more time for the children to complete the experience unhurriedly. While even experienced teachers want a basic curriculum, they do not follow it slavishly. They know that the danger in using a unit is that it may become stereotyped and forced. Then it can hinder real living at church.

The synopsis of the unit is the teacher's work chart as she guides the living of the group. A chart on the order of the following one is sometimes included with each unit in a Primary course of study.

Name of Unit

Scope ————

Teacher's Purpose (always in terms of the guidance of child purposing, thought, and activity)

Special Purposes	Problems	Materials from Which to Choose	Activities from Which to Choose
(Think in terms of guiding activity.)	(These problems are stated in terms of what children want to know, what they wonder about, purpose to do, think as they work.)	(Bible materials, poems, songs, stories, work materials, pictures, will be listed here.)	(These will be the activities that initiate, carry out, and judge the unit. They care for individual differences and varying maturities.)

Teachers planning together. The Primary teachers who use the unit of guided experience most effectively plan and work together. Superintendent, secretary, and pianist are teachers, just as class teachers or group leaders are. All of the Primary workers read carefully the entire unit that they are to teach. Then the teachers make their own plans on the basis of the ones in the course of study.

There are a number of ways in which Primary departments are now organized. These plans will be discussed in the companion book to this one, on Primary organization. This book discusses ways of organizing in order to make its suggestions on teacher planning clearer.

Most Primary children are now taught in three-grade departments, with a class for the six-year-olds, one for the seven-year-olds, and one for the eight-year-olds. Some of these departments use a separate course of study for each grade. Others use a departmental lesson. In such an organization all that has been said about the room can be, and is, used in many churches. Such a Primary department probably plans worship services for the children.

While each grade has its own course of study, it is surprising how often class activities and purposes can become departmental ones and how much of the departmental worship can be based on worship materials from the different grades. At times the third-grade plans will differ from those of first and second grades. In this case the third grade may worship by itself, if there are classrooms and departmental room, and the other two grades together. Some Primary departments that do not have separate classrooms plan trips for the younger children while the third grade worships, and vice versa. All sorts of plans are used to minister to older and younger children in ways that help them best to grow. The resourcefulness of teachers with limited equipment is a source of surprise and inspiration.

A second plan of organization for Primary children and for the Juniors is rapidly growing in favor. Instead of two departments with three grades each, three departments are provided for Primary and Junior children. The first is planned for six- and seven-year-old children, the second for eight- and nine-year-olds, and the third for the ten- and eleven-year-olds. One year of the course is used with the entire group at a time. Naturally it is harder to plan such an integrated program with three separate grades using three courses of study, but it is done successfully by many groups of Primary teachers. We shall consider planning under both forms of organization.

How a group might plan. Suppose the Christmas season is approaching. The Primary teachers plan to meet well in advance of the first Sunday in December. The superintendent asks each teacher to read the entire unit for December, both teacher's and pupil's materials. In addition, she asks each teacher to take a special assignment on which to report; or, in a three-grade department, one teacher in each grade will study the unit to see what stories, poems, and books are suggested. She will visit the public library to see what Christmas books are available for the reading table, will look over the departmental books for suitable ones. This same teacher looks through back issues for December of the story paper and binds suitable serial stories in attractive covers.

Another teacher will make a survey of community needs, especially of those to which the church contributes. Is there a clinic, a social center, a day nursery, a children's home, and so on, in the community or near by that needs the warm interest and friendly helpfulness of the group? She telephones, writes, or visits the workers to find just what is needed. In the light of the purposes and suggested activities in her teacher's book, she has practical suggestions ready for the teachers' conference. In a three-grade department she will consult teachers of each grade.

Then another teacher will study ways in which the children may enjoy the Christmas story. Who will tell the stories? Shall they be told to the entire group by the superintendent, or by the several teachers on succeeding Sundays, or will each teacher tell them to small groups? Can the children have a verse-speaking choir to use such a poetic telling of the Christmas story as "In Little Bethlehem"? How can carols be used to tell the Christmas stories? Will the children set up a crèche, a representation in objects of the Christmas story, and spontaneously dramatize it as they move the figures about? In a three-grade department each grade will assume a certain responsibility.

The pianist will study the music of each of the courses, or of the one course. From among the songs she will suggest several for the entire group to sing. She will prepare to teach them to the teachers at the workers' conference.

Pictures will be a special responsibility of another teacher. She will look through the departmental sets or files to select those that will be most suggestive of Christmas activities and worship. These will be on hand at the conference, and the teachers will study them together.

The secretary will check on available and needed materials.

At the meeting. At the time of the meeting the leader will see that purposes are reviewed for the month's work with the children.

Plan 1 (Two-Grade or Departmental Plan.) If the two-grade plan is followed and one year of the Closely Graded Course is used in cycle, or group or departmental courses are used, the workers will report in turn on their special assignments. Songs will be sung, books examined, activities chosen, pictures studied, ways of enjoying the Christmas story discussed. Then the workers will fill out a chart of what they hope to accomplish and will list activities and materials. They will use the chart in the teacher's book as a guide. The various leaders will choose the group plans that they wish to direct. A list of supplies will be made. These supplies will be secured by the secretary or the head teacher. Of course, the other leaders and the children may contribute to supplies under guidance of the one responsible.

Each teacher assumes responsibility for certain parts of the plan. One teacher may be responsible for a frieze; another for a trip; a third will tell the stories; a fourth, the pianist perhaps, will teach the songs; and so on. The leader discusses the purposes and shows how the plans and materials carry them out.

Then tentative plans for the entire first session will be made by all the leaders working together. The head teacher will be charged with special responsibility for group conferences and worship. These teachers are ready to guide children in a meaningful Christmas experience.

After teaching each session there is a brief checkup by all the teachers. Plans for the rest of the sessions are made in these brief meetings that occur at the end of each church-school session. The leader makes a copy of each plan to send to each teacher before the next Sunday. There is constant study of materials; reference to the group's plans; report on child contribution, response, and discovered need that change and enrich the plans. This plan was used for ten years by the leaders of one Primary group. They organized both environment and curriculum to accomplish the purposes that are discussed in Chapter I. Many other Primary groups have such meetings.

Plan 2 (for department with classes). If the Primary Department has three grades, the preparation is the same. The first step at the workers' conference is a meeting of the teachers of each grade. They should decide either to carry out special activities in each class within the grade or choose one large activity to which all classes will make a special contribution. For example, a third grade may wish to make illustrated books of Christmas carols, pose or dramatize Christmas carols, illustrate Christmas carols in a frieze or scene, and sing Christmas carols for some other group. Each class within the grade should work on *one* of the first three activities. The children should choose which group they will work with. All of them should take part in the last activity. Perhaps the time before the session will be used for it.

After grade meetings the entire group of teachers meet. Teachers of each grade tell their plans, and out of them or by their combination the departmental activities are chosen. Perhaps the third grade will be asked to set up the crèche for the entire group. Carol singing led by Grade 3 will become a departmental activity. The service activities f r Grades 1 and 2 may become the ones for the entire group. For example, one year a second grade who were learning the meaning of Christmas were trimming a tree with small red and green socks of money to send to a church that needed help in providing for children. Grade 3 helped to trim the tree and sent along its illustrated book of carols. Grade 1 was planning to fill a huge stocking for children in order to play Santa Claus. It went to the same group.

The superintendent and teachers will discuss what the emphasis should be each Sunday in the time for conference and worship. The service should be planned by teachers and superintendent together. They may decide that the Christmas stories from the Bible will be told to the entire group, not in the classes. Perhaps the superintendent will tell them; or she will tell one, and the teachers in turn will tell the others. There will never be more than one on any Sunday. In the class groups the teachers will be free to introduce poems for enjoyment and for use in verse speaking, as "I'm Wishing the Whole World Christmas." [4] Some of the children may wish to memorize Luke 2:8-14. There will be time for active group living in the classes accompanied by study and discussion. Unity, unhurriedness, and a richness of experience will be achieved for the entire group. The leaders will plan carefully to judge Christmas plans.

In a combined Beginners and Primary Department. Some teachers in a combined Beginners and Primary Department screen off a space for the younger group for the entire session. Others use a new grouping by placing the eight-year-olds in another group. If there are only a few children, then the plan for a double grade can be used provided eight-year-olds are cared for elsewhere and no children under four are enrolled. Very simple purposes and activities are planned for the younger children, and more advanced ones for the older ones. A great deal of individual guidance is needed. Even then the situation lacks value for the younger children.

The complete curriculum. With all the planning, adult leaders will not forget that the complete curriculum for Primary children at church consists of all experiences that the child has there. It is larger than the printed course of study. It is made up of place, people, plans, and source materials, all of which help leaders and children to live in greater good will, to seek and find fellowship with God, and to learn more of the Christian meaning of life.

Since children are a part of the group, they enter into the planning. Sometimes their contributions will mean a greatly enriched experience for both themselves and their leaders. Many a unit is doubled in length by the children's contributions. A fresh point of view may enter in; new needs may be uncovered; a complete reorganization of the leader's plan may be necessary. In such case the planning is not wasted.

---

[4] Annette Wynne, *More Silver Pennies*, The Macmillan Co., 1938, stanza 1.

Indeed, the children's contribution to their living and learning together would not have occurred with unprepared teachers who worked in individualistic or haphazard fashion.

FOR FURTHER STUDY

Starred books are for advanced study.

*Bower, W. Clayton. *The Curriculum of Religious Education.* New York: Charles Scribner's Sons, 1925. Chap. XI.

*Caswell, Hollis L., and Campbell, Doak S. *Curriculum Development.* New York: American Book Co., 1935. Pp. 378-99; Chaps. XV (esp. pp. 417-47), XVI.

*Coe, G. A. *Law and Freedom in the School.* Chicago: University of Chicago Press, 1924. Chap. IX.

Denominational literature on the Primary Department and the primary courses of study. Foreword in Part I of The Teacher's Book.

*Elliott, Harrison S. *Can Religious Education Be Christian?* New York: The Macmillan Co., 1940.

*Goggans, Sadie. *Units of Work and Centers of Interest in the Organization of the Elementary School Curriculum.* New York: Bureau of Publications, Teachers College, Columbia University, 1940. Chaps. II-IV.

Hockett, John A., and Jacobsen, E. W. *Modern Practices in the Elementary School.* Boston: Ginn & Co., 1938. Chaps. III, V.

Hockett, Ruth M., editor. *Teacher's Guide to Child Development.* Sacramento: California Department of Education, 1930. Chap. V. (Elementary.)

Lane, Robert H. *The Teacher in the Modern Elementary School.* Boston: Houghton Mifflin Co., 1941. Chap. IX.

Lee, J. Murray, and Lee, Doris M. *The Child and His Curriculum.* New York: D. Appleton-Century Co., 1940. Chaps. VI, VII.

McGaughy, J. R. *Classification of Pupils in the Elementary School.* New York: Progressive Education Association, 1941. (Pamphlet.)

Making of School Curricula, The. New York: Bureau of Publications, Teachers College, Columbia University. (Pamphlet.)

*Melvin, A. Gordon. *The Activity Program.* New York: The John Day Co., 1936. Chaps. III, V-VIII.

Minor, Ruby. *Early Childhood Education.* New York: D. Appleton-Century Co., 1937. Chap. XXI.

Storm, Grace E., and Smith, Nila B. *Reading Activities in the Primary Grades.* Boston: Ginn & Co., 1930. Chap. VII.

*Tiegs, Ernest W. *The Management of Learning in the Elementary Schools.* New York: Longmans, Green & Co., 1937. Chap. IX.

Use of Waste Materials. Washington: Association for Childhood Education. (Bulletin.)

FOR FURTHER ACTIVITY

1. Plan to spend at least half an hour in the Primary room. Reread pages 57-60 before you do so. Now make a list of ways in which your Primary room plans for the guidance of children. List ways in which it can be arranged to do so more fully.

2. If you entered a Primary room with few pictures, no work of the children in evidence, and the chairs arranged in a double semicircle facing the leader's table, how would you probably judge what went on in the room?

3. Add to the work chart suggested in Chapter II under "For Further Activity." Add columns, one to show activities and the other to show teaching materials. Keep this outline and, after teaching the unit, see how the plans changed in the teaching.

4. Suppose a visitor came while your children were working hard on plans that helped them both to express friendliness and to gain clearer ideas of God. After a while she grew restless and said, "I wonder when you will teach the lesson"—meaning "tell a story." Write how you would explain to her why you considered what they were doing the lesson on that Sunday.

5. Work out a plan for a teachers' meeting for your department. Even if very few teachers attend at first keep on with such planning and explain to them why it is so necessary. Are any changes in the work of the department noticeable after a year of such meetings? Keep a record of each meeting and of the work in the department. Has there been any change in the attitude of the teachers to one another?

6. Check over the supplies that are on hand. Are they suitable work materials to carry out the activities listed in the course of study you use?

to *before* class. In talk about the visit, by and questioning any of such features of the change, or of the children who work the class may have returned. The teacher had certainly questioned about the experiences. Later, also, she may keep relationships in those activities to interest. How children may work at church's activities to interest, how to help them to do their work at church.

Chapter IV

PLANNING TO TEACH

Placing the session in the unit. Chapter III discussed how a unit of guided experience parallels the action and development of a story and showed how some sessions initiate, some develop, and some evaluate and conclude the work of the class. So the first thing that the teacher does in preparing for a class period is to review the unit in her mind and see where the particular session may fit into it. She knows that no one session will stand by itself if the plans at church are made to guide children into more Christian ways of thinking, feeling, and acting.

Initiating or beginning sessions. Some sessions will be used to introduce a new unit of guided experience. Let us think of a unit of experience on work and worship at church. The teacher gains a clear understanding of her purposes. She makes a list of the ways her own group can take part in the work of the church. She thinks of all the other persons who work at church and of what they do. Then she plans how to guide the children so that they will become genuinely interested in having a part in the work of the church.

The time has come to plan the first session. Perhaps she decides that a trip to certain parts of the church building will be a good way to start. The children will use a few minutes to look at pictures of different parts of the building. They will decide to visit them. They will discuss ways of acting on a trip. The rest of this session will be given to the trip itself. At the end of it the teacher may repeat a poem, like "The church, it always seems to me," to add meaning to what the group has seen and done. She may suggest that next Sunday they will find out more about their church.

The unit is not yet initiated. So, for the second session,

the teacher plans to talk about the trip, to call attention to any special features of the church, or to any church workers the class may have seen. This plan should lead to listing questions about the church and the workers there. The teacher may tell a story or show a picture to suggest how children may work at church. The group may ask God to help them to do their work at church.

These are only two kinds of beginning sessions. The course of study may suggest others that are much more valuable than any the teacher can think of. Some of them might be: showing objects and pictures and having a picture study, teaching a hymn, telling a story. Sometimes the children start a unit by what they bring or by the questions they ask. At other times conversation about an approaching festival or some unusual event or just about daily happenings may launch the children on a new line of living and discovery. All of these new plans introduce new problems and help children to set up new purposes.

Developmental sessions. At other times the teacher's plan will help children to carry out purposes and solve problems or gain new insights. These are the class periods that come after the initiating ones. In them experience is developed and enriched and at last brought to a successful conclusion. In all these sessions the teacher uses stories, poems, Bible verses, pictures, and objects to add insight and meaning in the midst of the class living. She helps the children to move on through the unit. Of course, a completely logical development does not follow in work with children. New interests arise, new purposes and plans.

After each session the teacher asks herself: "What comes next, if I build on what happened today? Which of the plans in the teacher's book are most helpful and practical for my class? Which ones are most needed by my children? How have the children changed the plans?" She may choose a poem that will add religious meaning to the work of the class. Then she realizes that there will be no time to use a story also. So she weighs the value of each in terms of child religious growth and makes her choice between the two. Step by step, session by session, the teacher carefully plans to guide her boys and girls so that her purposes for their religious growth and theirs for class living are realized. She is careful not to add so much material or so many plans that the children have no time to think and to feel.

Judging or concluding sessions. The last kind of session plan brings the class to the point where they sum up and judge for themselves what they have done and learned. Usually many of the new problems and purposes that lead to the next unit of guided experience arise at this time. To summarize, each class period is planned to contribute to the development of experience and to make its proper contribution to the religious growth of the members of the class.

Time to get ready. Many Primary teachers have reported that they make their first study of the plan for the next session just as soon as possible. The needs, interests, and contributions of the children are fresh in mind at this time. Also the leaders have plenty of time to prepare. Good teaching of children requires materials for boys and girls to work with. The teacher checks on what will be needed to carry out the work. Then she secures it.

Some teachers, especially when they are learning to teach, try out activities ahead of time so that they will know just how to proceed. A second grade planned to make a peep show of an Oriental house. The teacher had no idea of how to make one. "My hands are so clumsy that I'll never get it done." But just the same she decided to carry out the directions in her teacher's book. She assembled the materials, made a peep show, and furnished it. In telling about her experiment she said, "Then I destroyed it so that I would not be tempted to use it as just a model or do the work myself for the children." This teacher said that she had learned how to guide the children, what materials to use, and how to use them. Of course, she did not continue to go to such pains as she grew in teaching skill; but her ability to lead Primary children came from her first hard work. Experienced teachers often plan for two or three different kinds of activities so that the children may choose among them. It is wise for the learning teacher at first to work out one plan and stick to it.

Early planning also allows time for the teacher to master teaching materials of a literature type, or pictures, or other materials. The teacher can tell her story several times during the week, or she may work out a plan for using a poem and memorize the poem. She may make plans to teach a hymn and learn to sing it. She may study a picture and plan her conversation about it. She may think of possible class prayers and of what petitions they may contain. When teachers plan carefully and thoughtfully, the Primary children are safe with them.

Child responsibility. The boys and girls should be encouraged to contribute to the plans also. Sometimes definite jobs will be given them. In this case the mother should know just what is expected. Sometimes a plan may depend for its success on a member of the group. If the child forgets or does not carry out his part, the teacher should not do it for him. Children learn to be responsible and dependable at church when they realize in their very bones what a failure to do one's part means.

Children should always feel that they are free to bring and share what they can. They should know that their ideas are always wanted and may change and improve the teacher's plans. One Christmas a Primary group were interested in pictures of the swaddled Baby that they found in a book. "Could we fix our babies like that?" the little girls asked. "If you bring them, I'll bring the cloth and the tape," the teacher answered. The next Sunday she took squares cut from an old sheet. Fifteen little girls appeared with dolls. They were very lovely on Christmas Sunday with the swaddled dolls. They sang "Come Softly, Tread Gently," as a lullaby.

Personal contacts add informality. It is fine for the teacher to plan carefully for a class period. Yet more is needed than even such thoughtfulness. Every child has his peculiar religious needs and wonderings. He should feel that his teacher understands and plans for him, that he has an important place in the group. His special abilities are recog-

nized and used. Ralph was always restless and often a disturb-
ing influence in his class. Then one day his teacher discovered
that he could write the brief titles or stories to go in a book or
on a chart or frieze better than she could. Ralph became very
responsible and gave little trouble after that.

Often the individual's need will require that the teacher
help him outside of the church. She may work with his parents. She may have him in her home. She seeks to share with
such a child all her living trust and experience of God. This
is true child winning for the kingdom of God. A record of
how Primary teachers in Christian churches are nurturing
and guiding the boys and girls would be an inspiring one.
It is a silent, unseen service that few persons ever know
about. Yet it is the real evangelism for these children, and it
brings its reward to these teachers in the religious growth
of their children.

Prepare to change your plans. When Primary children
live and learn with their church-school teacher, they will make
many unexpected contributions. So will their parents. It has
been my experience that teaching that is guidance of growth
brings a fine co-operation from most parents.

At first unexpected additions to the session confuse the
teacher. "I never did teach my lesson," she may be tempted
to think in a disturbed sort of way. However, when she
checks on what actually happened, she finds that she accom-
plished all that she had planned or more, even if she reached
her goal in a very unexpected way. In time the teacher realizes
that parents, children, and teacher working together achieve
purposes that could not be realized in any other way.

Plan with the other teachers. Every teacher in a Primary group is a member of a fellowship, the entire teaching
staff of the Primary department. So far as possible, plans
should be made in conference. Successful teaching comes
with understanding among the teachers. Large, important
activities are possible only when each teacher fits her plans
into a larger one and each class works on some special part
of the plan.

There is a more important reason for joint planning than

teaching efficiency and guidance of important activities. The children should feel that there is fellowship among the teachers, that they practice Christian brotherliness among themselves. It may seem easier for the superintendent to plan her work by herself and for each teacher to work in individualistic fashion; but, so long as they do, an essential quality in religious teaching is lacking.

To see how well teachers can plan together and to get an idea of how practical and definite they make their plans, let us study some excerpts from a teacher's notebook. These plans were used with a third- and fourth-grade group in a vacation church school where the children were learning to contrast Bible homes with homes today. The first session initiated the work.

SESSION I

1. Arrange room in interesting centers. There will be:

   a) *A picture center,* with a Telebinocular,[1] pictures of Palestinian life, and pictures of modern home life (especially those of occupations and activities of fathers, mothers, and children);

   b) *An objects center,* with Palestinian sheep bell, sling, and mezuzah;

   c) *A supplies center,* with large sign ("We Shall Be Busy This Summer"), roll of wrapping paper, clay in a small covered garbage can or stone jar, tempera paints and easel, crayons, scissors, large pieces of construction paper, and paste;

   d) *A book center,* with such books as *Hebrew Home Life* by Lobingier, *Ruth* by the Petershams, *Peter's Family* by Hanna, *The Smiths and Rusty* by Dalgliesh, *Esa, Little Boy of Nazareth,* by Neville, *Isaac of the Tents* by Entwistle, *Bible Stories to Read* by Moore, *Little Town* by the Haders, and *Little House* by Burton;

   e) *A music center.* Pianist will play softly "The Home God Gave to Me."

2. Children, on arrival, move around in centers; teachers are at hand to answer questions.

3. A conference of the entire group is held.

   a) Leader uses part of poem "What Makes a Home?" by Grace N. Crowell, to arouse children's conscious appreciation for homes and to start a discussion.

   b) They sing "The Home God Gave to Me."

   c) Leader says: "You have seen this morning that all people do

---

An electric stereoscope, made by Keystone Co., Meadville, Pa.

not live as you do. What did you learn?" Children report. Bring
in reports from other sources. Entire group looks at some large
appropriate pictures of home life.

d) Questions come from the group about ways of living in Palestine. Leader makes a list and plans with group to post it as a guide
for plans and work.

e) One teacher tells a story of a family who went to visit in
Palestine. She tells the children that we are so interested in the
country because Jesus once lived there, but makes clear that it is
helpful, too, just to see how other people live, in ways like or different from our own.

f) They sing "Tell Me the Stories of Jesus," stanza 1.

g) Group plays a game of Palestinian children mentioned in story,
and some of their own games.

h) Children imagine themselves in Palestine—eat dates and hard
crackers.[2]

It will be seen that this session provides a stimulating
environment, leads to questions that the children decide to
answer, introduces the element of contrast, and furnishes a
variety of source materials and experiences.

SESSION II

This session helps the children to continue to purpose and
to choose plans, to carry out their purpose of contrasting
Bible homes with homes today.

1. The list of questions is posted on a chart.
2. There is activity at the centers.

a) In the *book center* the teacher begins to read *The Smiths and
Rusty*, or *Esa. Silver Pennies* is also on table. She may read "Animal
Crackers" by Morley. Some children read for themselves.

b) At the supplies center there has been added a box of pictures
that contrast American home life with that in Palestine at the time
of Jesus. There is also a large carton. A table near by holds a long
strip of paper, tempera paints, and brushes.

3. Children examine environment as before. One child brings a book
that shows a picture of a tent. It is placed in the picture center. Ralph
and George bring some Palestinian costumes out of the supply closet
with the suggestion that a play be given. Leader asks, "What play?"
Boys say, "We could find out. Can we read the books?"

4. In conference children review their questions and add others.

[2] To use this plan in a Sunday session, use 2 in the presession and omit 3-*e*,
f, *g*, and perhaps *h*.

They discuss plans for working out their study. Interest or work groups are set up.

a) Some children choose to make a tent home on lawn of church. (This activity has been introduced through pictures.)

b) Some plan to make a village home. Leader shows pictures and calls attention to a box that might be used for a peep show.

c) Some wish to make a play. Begin to study books. Ask a teacher to read to them. Some read for themselves.

d) Some fourth-grade children wish to make contrast charts on occupations and activities.

5. They sing "Morning Hymn," stanza 2, and pray, asking that work may go well. They sing "The Home God Gave to Me."

6. Interest or work groups are busy.

7. One mother sends lemonade and cookies. Teacher speaks with appreciation of how friendly mothers are.

It will be seen that the above session was for purposing and planning. The next session continued plans and enriched them.

SESSION III

1. There is more activity at the centers.

a) Tent group size up their place on lawn. Consult books and pictures. Listen to story of Abraham and Lot. Go down town to get lumber and sacking for tent. Make interesting contacts with merchants. Ask about Palestinian merchants. Add questions to the list.

b) Peep show group start work on box. Realize their need to divide into two groups, one to work on house and people, one on furnishings. Consult pictures and research charts to see how to work, what to make.

2. Later all groups have a conference.

a) Tent group shows a picture of Abraham and Lot. Leader speaks of them as shepherds.

b) Pianist plays "He Shall Feed His Flock" from Handel's *Messiah*. Children and leader have appreciative music experience.

c) Leader shows a shepherd's pipe. Children add to objects. They decide to add others to make an exhibit table. One boy promises a necklace with a Bethlehem star.

3. Group has a playtime.

The teacher's notebook goes on to describe how planning sessions continued and purposes were worked out. New interests entered. One day the leader took the children to a wheat farm. They took along a hand sickle and contrasted it with a modern combine. They saw grain standing in the corners of the field. The leader read Leviticus 19 to them. They talked about how hungry people are cared for now. They decided they would like to help. They learned "The Song of the Bread." [3]

As they found answers to their questions, they checked them off the list.

These were planning and working sessions, and new purposes arose also. The experience was enriched because a member of the congregation lent a beautiful robe from Palestine.

Then the last sessions were summarizing and evaluating sessions. The interest groups were about through their work. They had grown quite friendly with a Chinese girl in the neighborhood. The leader suggested that the children share with her what they were learning and doing. The group asked that their parents be included also. They planned invitations, exhibit, and program. In the interest groups they checked on work to see what remained to be done. They checked their questions to see which were unanswered. Some new ones arose. These were to be kept for a new experience. The final session came. The children shared their work. They asked riddles that contrast occupations. They had their dramatization and a Palestinian dramatic game for visitors.

Characteristics of all session plans. It will be seen that what happens in a session plan is determined by where the group is in living and learning. One session takes up where the last one left off. There is rich but unhurried experience, an active thought-provoking life. Children and teachers have fun together. They are studying, working, playing, laughing, and worshiping together. When behavior problems arise, the leaders take the attitude of physicians. They try not to judge a child but to find his need and to release him so far as possible from strain or fear to a sense of his own worth and of his responsibility for the group. Many "bad" children are very unhappy or fearful. Both teachers and children grow in a sense of social responsibility and find stability in the

[3] *Graded Courses, Primary Bible Folder*, Course II, No. 40. Adapted from Grace Wilbur Conant, *The Children's Year*, Milton Bradley Co.

worship of God. Both use their abilities in ways that are constructive and stimulating.

Such a fully developed plan suits the vacation school and the expanded session. In the Sunday church school with a session sixty minutes in length the same kind of session plan will be used because the same child learns in the same way on Sunday. The plan will be simplified to fit the shorter period. The unit will take more class periods. Fewer activities will be attempted and not so many enriching experiences will be possible. This is the only difference.

Certain general principles. Regardless of the time schedule—vacation church school, expanded session, Sunday church school—and of the organization—class, combined Beginners and Primary, grade, two-grade, department with three grades—the leaders will follow certain principles:

1. All teachers should plan together. Superintendent and teachers are equally responsible for the children. No superintendent can be successful unless she has a thorough knowledge of each unit in the course of study. She should help the teachers to use them. The fellowship of Christian leaders lends a religious quality over and above the skill that it adds to teaching.

2. The teachers study their materials thoroughly. They will have a clear mastery of purposes and see how these purposes work out in the sessions.

3. They will use the materials to guide children, not as the end in themselves. A unit of work can be a presentation of materials unless the teacher realizes that her task is to guide children, not to teach a certain amount of material. She remembers that human life alone is capable of being religious, that books are religious only because they record experiences of religion and of revelations of God that help other people to be religious.

4. The teacher adapts the printed plans in her teacher's book to the religious needs of her own class. She reorganizes, expands, shortens, and even omits some of the units in the course of study in the light of the group's needs and interests.

5. In the long run, any good course of study is a record

of successful teaching by experienced persons and so should help superintendents and the teachers by suggesting suitable problems, activities, source materials, and an organization of activity and materials into teaching plans and procedures.

6. Teachers check on their supplies and see that they are available. They encourage the children to bring materials and supplies. They work with the children to keep supplies in easily available and neat condition. Probably the superintendent or the secretary will be primarily responsible for securing supplies. Every teacher should be on the lookout for materials to contribute.

7. Teachers make careful plans, but they hold themselves ready to change. That is, they accept and follow the children's contributions and leads whenever they make a contribution.

8. Teachers and children see whatever they start through to a conclusion.

9. They thoughtfully summarize, evaluate, and share their learnings.

Summary. It will be seen that planning to teach a session at church is planning for rich, stimulating, and friendly group living and that teachers, including superintendent and other officers, work together. Purpose are kept clearly in mind, and the kind of environment in which Primary children learn to grow as Christians is supplied. Responsibility and perseverance are encouraged, and individual personality problems are expected and met in ways that help personality to integrate increasingly around Christian values. The rich religious heritage of Christian people is used intrinsically: that is, it is woven in as a part of group living. The teacher studies, plans, works with other teachers, knows her children and their religious needs.

FOR FURTHER STUDY

Books starred are for advanced study.

*Caswell, Hollis L., and Campbell, Doak S. *Curriculum Development.* New York: American Book Co., 1935. Chap. XII (esp. pp. 358-61).

*Coe, George A. *What Is Christian Education?* New York: Charles Scribner's Sons, 1929. P. 123.

*Goggans, Sadie. *Units of Work and Centers of Interest in the Organization of the Elementary School Curriculum.* New York: Bureau of Publications, Teachers College, Columbia University, 1940.

Helping Children to Work Alone. Washington: Association for Childhood Education. (Bulletin.)

Hockett, John A., and Jacobsen, E. W. *Modern Practices in the Elementary School.* Boston: Ginn & Co., 1938. Chap. II.

Hockett, Ruth M., editor. *Teacher's Guide to Child Development.* Sacramento: California Department of Education, 1930. (Elementary.)

Lane, Robert H. *The Teacher in the Modern Elementary School.* Boston: Houghton, Mifflin Co., 1941. Chap. V.

McLester, Frances Cole. *Teaching in the Church School.* Nashville: Abingdon-Cokesbury Press, 1940. Chaps. IV, VI, X.

*Melvin, A. Gordon. *The Activity Program.* New York: The John Day Co., 1936. Chaps. XII, XII-XV.

Trends in Unit Teaching. New York: New York State Association of Elementary Principals, Bulletin II, September, 1934.

Washburne, Carleton W. *A Living Philosophy of Education.* New York: The John Day Co., 1940. Chap. XXIII.

*Young, W. E., editor. *The Social Studies in the Elementary School.* Twelfth Yearbook, National Council for the Social Studies, N. E. A., 1941.

FOR FURTHER ACTIVITY

1. Write your week-by-week plans in a notebook. Use one page and leave the opposite page to record what happens in class: what you do, what the children do and say, needs of children, ways children change plans. Keep this record for every session for at least three months.

2. Write in three hundred words what you have learned from this chapter and from Chapter III, about planning class sessions.

3. Answer these questions about the next session plan in your teacher's book:

   a) How does it help to realize your purposes?

   b) How much of it can you use in your class?

   c) What special needs of your class will it help to meet?

   d) Is it an introductory, developmental, or concluding session?

   e) Make your own plan based on the one in the book.

4. Contrast in five hundred words a "lesson" such as church-school teachers once used with a session plan as developed in this chapter.

5. How would you help the following teachers? Be practical.

   a) The teacher who says, "I can't use this activity because I haven't time to assemble the materials."

b) The teacher who says, "If I use this activity, there will be no time to teach the lesson."

c) The superintendent who says, "I never can get my teachers together to plan. We live so far apart. I have to do it all."

6. What is the place of the Bible in these session plans?

7. Why should the teacher work for a spirit of informal friendliness? How does it nurture children religiously?

8. Tell how the teacher's sense of the reality of God colors all the session plan.

9. In what ways does Christian teaching require more than careful planning and skillful use of method?

Chapter V

GROWING RELIGIOUSLY THROUGH
EXPERIENCES WITH LITERATURE

THE first picture that comes to mind when the title of this chapter is read may be one of a teacher telling stories to a group of children. Storytelling is still one of the helpful uses of literature with Primary children, provided the teacher uses the method with an understanding of what it is, what its limitations are, what other uses of literature are just as valuable, and if she knows how to use the method well.

The value of the story. A story is helpful when it broadens experience and lends religious meaning to everyday life. It is especially helpful to the third grade when it lifts them out of the here and now into the here and there, and, in the simplest fashion, into the now and then. The story may also suggest good activities to Primary boys and girls and may offer, at times, solutions for daily problems. It can bring fun to a group or lift group living to a climax in worship. It may bind the group together through a shared understanding or by giving an enriched sense of unity.

What is a story? Someone has said that a story is a picture of life caught in an art form. In the story some problem is solved, some tensions relieved, or some purpose achieved. Through stories the children learn to know people who have lived and learned, wondered, made discoveries, known God, and served their fellowmen.

Storytelling is only one way of guiding children through the use of literature. While it is an enjoyable one, a variety of experiences with literature, associated with religious ideas and friendly ways of acting, is necessary. If the teacher uses storytelling exclusively with children, she lowers her teaching to the level of mere entertainment and telling. She leaves too much of the children's religious guidance to chance.

Telling a new Bible story every Sunday is a sure way to use some unsuitable stories and to confuse the children about all Bible stories. The Primary teachers do not wish to see the church become a place where children are introduced too rapidly to religious materials. They are eager to gain skill in using only well-selected and suitable Bible stories, to use other helpful literature from the Bible, and to know and use other selections from children's literature that will contribute to the children's experience of religion.

How to tell stories. Storytelling should be artistic. The teacher should have a clear purpose in mind, and yet the story should not moralize. It carries its own message. The story should have plenty of action that starts in an interesting beginning. This beginning should give the setting, introduce characters and problem, and set the action in progress. The story should develop through a series of steps that rise to a climax, both in action and in emotion. The climax should solve the problem. Then the end should complete the action and leave the hearer at rest.

Stories achieve their effect by such art methods as contrast and repetition. The Good Samaritan is an excellent example of the use of both. The old folk and fairy tales yield other excellent examples. They are well known to all of us. This contrast and repetition is carried out in characters, in setting, in action. For example, the act of the Good Samaritan is contrasted with that of priest and Levite. There is a triple repetition of opportunity and response.

Sometimes the contrast is in the emotional quality induced by the setting. There is Maud Lindsay's story "The Harper." When the harper struggles through to his home at last, the very elements reflect his achievement. "The snow ceased its falling, the wind its blowing, and the harper saw before him the open doorway of his own home." The very setting means peace, security, warmth, and light, after struggle, cold, and darkness.

Sometimes the action has cumulative effect. *Ask Mr. Bear*, by Marjorie Flack, is such a story. Sometimes the action piles up through repetition of the same experience with different people or creatures. All of them add additional insight for the child. *Pelle's New Suit,* by Elsa Beskow, is an example.

The rhyming couplet is also used to achieve unity and effect. "The Road That Wanted to Be Beautiful," by Carolyn S. Bailey, is a charming story for older Primary children because of the repeated verse Wake, wake, for the brow. road's sake.

The ending of a story should give a child a sense of assurance that the problem is really solved. There should be an element of child mastery in it. Children give a little movement of triumph when they come to the end of "How the Singing Water Got into the Tub," by Lucy Sprague Mitchell. Dorothy Baruch's stories for the preschool child—as, for instance, *The Two Bobbies*—magnificently achieve such an ending.

The stories should be within the range of the child's interest. Then they are stuff to nurture living. They should be about other children and their activities. One of the most joyous worship experiences of young Primary children I ever saw resulted from playing in and gathering autumn leaves on the church lawn. They were to be pressed and waxed. This activity was followed by the use of the story "Lost in the Leaves" [1] and the poem "I Like the Woods in Autumn." [2] "God Giveth Us Richly All Things to Enjoy" was sung. "Lord of the Sunlight" was used as a prayer.

Stories should show children successfully solving their problems in order that their free and joyous activity can go on. This is the hardest of all stories to tell, for it must not moralize. It must take an objective note and must center its emphasis on the joy that comes as a result of the difficult achievement. One of the best stories of this type for the first grade is "When Fun Begins." [3]

The Bible story. The Bible story for Primary children should be carefully chosen to help the children to learn and

---

[1] From *Told Under the Blue Umbrella,* The Macmillan Co.
[2] From *Sung Under the Silver Umbrella,* The Macmillan Co., 1935.
[3] From Pearl S. Buck, *Stories for Little Children,* The John Day Co., 1940.

to grow. It should not be told just for purposes of instilling knowledge of the Bible. The limitations of Primary children should be kept in mind in its selection and telling. Because they have no historical sense, these children profit little from Old Testament stories that reflect a pre-Christian concept of God. Many New Testament stories are difficult of understanding also. Yet the teacher does real violence to the majesty of the Bible record when she simplifies the stories to the point of triviality or positive misinterpretation just to be able to use a Bible story.

The Bible story will be used to encourage the life of good will. The friendliness of Jesus may be learned through a number of stories of his ministry. The story may interpret great festivals of the Christian year. It may help the children the better to understand God, to enter more fully into his service and to worship him.

Primary teachers should realize that far more than through stories, the Christian religion is made manifest for Primary children through the lives of adults whom they trust. The age for serious Bible study has not yet arrived. The Bible stories that are most important for Primary children have been discussed on pages 33-34.

Now let us turn to other kinds of literature that make a contribution to the religious living of Primary children. We shall discuss ways to use each one. The lyric poem, books, and the literature that children make themselves will be included.

Poems. Poets are very close to childhood, for they retain in adult life a blessed childlikeness. So they can truly "pipe for children." All great children's poets might say as Blake did:

> And I wrote my happy songs
> Every child may joy to hear.

Poets add meaning to life. They express their swift, sure insight in word pictures that are sensory, playful, and social. To read good children's poetry is to learn much of children. To share it with them is to build up a most unusual fellowship with the boys and girls.

The poem is one of the most valuable forms of literature for Primary children, especially in guiding worship and in times of group intimacy and fun. Many a disciplinary problem vanishes when the parent or teacher uses some poem that is seemingly irrelevant but has delightful associations for child or group. So teachers may rejoice that there are so many excellent poems for children today.

Primary teachers will wish to look for a moment at some poems that have been used with children. Sometimes the poem may be used instead of a less suitable story or song to guide children into a time of wonder, appreciation, or worship. One Primary leader selected Walter de la Mare's "Silver" and Eleanor Farjeon's "The Sounds in the Morning" to lead children to sense the rhythm of day and night. The children told dreamily of how they had seen all the world silvered under the moonlight. There was a brisk movement in the group when the second poem was introduced. The Bible verse, "The day is thine, the night also is thine," was the prayer. This worship experience used only this material for its fine effect.

Once when the children had been learning about workers and were thinking of men as interdependent, the leader said, "See if you know these workers." She read the following poems: "The Barber's," by Walter de la Mare; "General Store" and "The Florist Shop," by Rachel Field. The reading was accompanied by delightful, spontaneous conversation about the children's own experiences with those people. The group had a sense of grateful unity with all of them when they sang:

> We're glad, O God, that it is true
> That children can be workers, too.
> Thank you, God, for workers.

Poems can lend meaning to childlike activities. Once a second grade was making a bulb garden. The children were working on a small flower bed just outside the room. They talked about the bulbs, how to plant them, how they would lie dormant until certain things happened—such as a proper amount of rain, sun, warmth—how the sleep in the cold earth was necessary that beautiful blossoms might come. "It's like a plan," said Jean. "It is a plan," the teacher said quietly. "Things just don't happen all jumbled together without any meaning. There is a plan for everything that lives and grows." Then she used the poem "The Little Brown Bulbs." [4] With a note of triumph it traces the entire process from planting to blossoming and tells how the daffodils worshiped at Easter. Several times during the winter the children asked about the poem. It was repeated. They ran out to see their garden at regular intervals. Then one glorious day the children saw the first sign of green. "They've jumped out of bed," they called to the teacher. Later some of them asked to learn the poem so that they could say it for the aged people to whom they carried flowers on Easter day.

Sometimes children like to repeat poems as they work. The poem adds meaning to the activity. A second grade repeated "I Like the Woods in Autumn" as they waxed autumn leaves to decorate their room and later to share with a Primary group, in lower California, who never saw leaves change.

Sometimes a poem helps an older Primary child to understand a custom or practice of another race or culture in delightful fashion. One teacher placed a mezuzah on the table when her third grade were contrasting Bible home life and customs with their own. She answered the children's questions about what it was. She showed them the Bible verse that was written on the tiny enclosed scroll. She told how Jews of long ago and of today place it on the doorpost. "But why?" asked Russell. "What makes them?" Then the teacher read them "The Sign on the Doorpost," from *When He Was Just a Little Child,* by Lucy Diamond. The children asked her to make a large chart of Deuteronomy 6:4-5. Using the chart, the children drilled themselves on the verse. Sometimes two children would be seen helping one another to learn it. The children placed the mezuzah on the door of their own room and touched it as they went in and out. "What do you

think when you do that?" the teacher asked. She did not wish
this to be artificial mimic play. "Why," said Joe, "I think
. . ." and he repeated the Shema.

Sometimes a poem can help children to express that ex-
pansiveness of emotion that is so normal an accompaniment
of their successful experiences. One Christmas the third
grade had been enjoying Christmas carols and customs from
many lands. They had made a crèche. They were singing
carols for their pastor that night. They were full of good
will. The leader read the first stanza of Annette Wynne's
"I'm Wishing the Whole World Christmas." The children
asked for it several times; and one boy flung out his arms
as he repeated, "I'm wishing the whole world Christmas."
For a moment the group had sensed what a world brotherhood rejoicing over Advent meant.

The poetry of the Bible can mean much to Primary children when it is used by a teacher who is stirred to worship
by it. One morning a group took a walk to a little lane that
they loved. Spring had come unheralded during the week.
The children looked at the teachers with delighted and
startled eyes. "This is the Lord's doing. It is marvelous in
our eyes," the leader said softly; and then the group was
silent for a moment. They went back to work. These children
had known the very heart of communion with God.

The Bible is a highly poetic book even if much of its
beauty is hidden in translation. This is natural, for Hebrew
is a picturesque language and the Jews were a passionate
people whose motive and mainspring was their yearning after
God and the meaning of life. Such a combination means
poetic expression.

Ways to use poems. The teacher's purpose in using a
poem and the kind of poem chosen help determine the method
of using it. Devotional poetry from the Bible may be introduced simply at that moment when it will lead children to
worship.

A first grade tended a cocoon all winter. In March the
moth emerged while the children were at church. The group
watched the struggles of the tiny damp creature. They saw

the moth in all his beauty. "This is the Lord's doing; it is marvelous in our eyes," quoted the teacher in a quiet voice. The next Sunday this verse was written with black crayon on a large sheet of paper and pinned to a screen. The children illustrated it with pictures that showed the growth cycle of a moth. They worshiped through the use of the verse. There are many poetic verses in the Bible that can be used to lead children to see religious meaning in daily experience.

A second grade had just packed a box for an Indian school. They dictated a letter to the Indian children. Then the teacher said: "When I think of our letter, I remember a poem. It speaks of a letter as a gypsy elf. I think that means a fairy that wanders around from place to place. Isn't that a nice way to speak of a letter? Let's see what this gypsy elf, the letter, does and where it goes." Then she repeated the poem "A Letter Is a Gypsy Elf," by Annette Wynne. The children delightedly traced the letter on its trip to the Indians. The last two lines were repeated again and again. "This gypsy elf will find good friends," chuckled Patsy.

A difficult poem needs more of an introduction. One teacher introduced "Bible Stories," by Lizette Woodworth Reese, in this way to her third grade. She told of a writer, a poet, who loved a room in her home when she was a child. It was a living room. It seemed so cozy that she thought of it as a kind room. The chairs had black seats with gold roses embroidered upon them. There were lovely teacups with rims of gold. Her mother told the little girl Bible stories in such a splendid way that she made her see the people in them. She thought she could see David as a lad walking across her father's fields. She called them "acres old." She imagined that the Little Jesus came to supper with her. Then she read the poem to the children. There was a moment of silence at the end. Then the teacher said: "If the people in the Bible were living now, which ones would you like to have visit you?" The children told of their favorite Bible people and why they would invite them.

The Primary teacher should have many Bible verses of devotional character and many children's poems at her command to use as they fit in. Usually the poems should be spoken, not read. However, if a poem is needed, the teacher should not hesitate to read it.

She should understand the spirit and meaning of each poem and repeat it in such a way that the children understand. Often this interpretation requires a slight pausing or a slight emphasis on certain words. One whiny, quarrelsome child in vacation church school was helped to get a perspective on himself when the teacher read in a spirit of fun, "The Camel's Lament." When she came to the lines,

> There's never a question about my digestion
> Anything does for me,

she used a whiny, injured tone. "What a dope," the boy chuckled. Afterwards a twinkle in the teacher's eye and a softly murmured, "Anything does for me," would pull the boy right out of himself. The moral value of this poem is about as completely absent as possible, but it helped one boy to find himself.

Another Primary teacher was disturbed at Easter by the selfish cruelty that her children practiced toward little animals and fowl. In the midst of an excited recital about ducks, colored chickens, and rabbits for Easter, she quietly repeated "A Fairy Went A-Marketing," by Rose Fyleman. There was no comment. The next day some of the children said, "Tell us about the kind fairy again." "Yes," added several others, "she was so kind." The teacher was nonplussed. "What fairy do you mean?" she was about to ask when one child said, "I liked the part about, 'And then she kissed his silken ears.' " The teacher repeated the poem again. There was a silence. Then Tom said slowly, "I don't believe you are glad about the chickens and the rabbits and the ducks." The teacher then asked, "Did you get any new ideas of how to treat your Easter bunnies and ducks and chickens?" Several parents later thanked the teacher. A number of children stopped asking for live creatures, and others were more kindly.

The poems children make. When a teacher is sensitive to child life and to the world about her, children naturally express themselves in poetry. The teacher can help by making children conscious of some of the experiences that they are having. One Sunday a soft, fluffy snow accompanied by frost made the whole landscape a fairyland. The children came into the Primary room stirred by the beauty. The teacher did not refer to it until the children did. "It's like a hush," said Mary. Afterwards she wrote:

> The frost has made a soft white wonderland.
> It is so still, I say "Hush, hush";
> Then I think,
> I think of God.

One first-grade Primary teacher kept a book to record the children's poetic reactions to their experiences. She herself had a sensitive appreciation of life. Her own insight and her anticipation of their ability to express themselves poetically stimulated them to do so. The class book recorded these poems:

> This morning as I came to school
> I saw the gold tree that we sat under.
> It was so pretty to me.
> The leaves were off at the top.
> They had dropped like a tick-tock to the ground,
> Making a golden crown for the ground.
> The leaves will keep falling off like rain
> Till they are all on the ground
> And not a one on the tree.

> > Here is a little tree.
> > It's fall colors.
> > It's green,
> > It's brown,
> > It's red,
> > It's yellow.
> > Oh, oh, oh!
> > How did it get that way? [5]

A second grade wrote this song. It was the result of many experiences of wonder and worship. It grew out of their study of and interest in the seasons.

[5] First grade, practice school, Memphis State Teachers College. The first was written by a group, the second by an individual. Used by courtesy of Miss Suiter, the teacher.

Winter, summer, spring, and fall
Earth is spinning like a ball.
Ice and cold the winter brings.
In the springtime robin sings.

Swimming all the summer days,
Autumn leaves fall from the trees.
Happy children run and play
Every season, every day.

A child brought this poem to her teacher at church one Sunday just before Christmas:

It is Christmas, Christmas now;
The shepherds hear the angel song;
They see the Little, Little Baby.
It is Christmas, Christmas now.

Another child of eight years asked one day, "Do you ever wonder?" "O yes," was the answer. Then she showed this poem:

I WONDER

I wonder why the trees bend in the autumn wind;
I wonder why their leaves turn red;
I wonder why the birds fly high;
I wonder, "Does God know about them all?"

At Easter, Martha wrote:

On Easter Day
I saw a bluebird.
He sang to me
From a soft green tree.
The flowers were blooming, too,
And the sun was sunning them all.

A second-grade child wrote:

THIS IS AUTUMN TIME

All the world is beautiful.
This is autumn time.
Leaves of fire,
Leaves of gold,
Birds fly south
Away from cold.
World is like a rainbow.
This is autumn time.

The public school helps the child to grow in the use of the language arts. It also helps him to gain insight into life and to express wonder and appreciation. The church school shares the second and third purposes with the public school and adds the additional purpose of helping children to grow articulate in worship. These are the reasons why religious teachers help children to express themselves in poetry.

The teacher should read the work of the great children's poets. She will notice their objectivity, their freedom from condescension and preachiness, their heightening of sensory and social experience, and their joyousness. Their sense of wonder is a spiritual approach to life. The teacher will also notice that they avoid analogy and symbolism of the kind not understood by children.

The book corner. The book corner should be one of the most important centers of happy living in the Primary room. It may be only an orange crate or even a few books on a window ledge in some small church with limited equipment. It may be an open bookcase with chairs placed invitingly near by. There may be a table. If the books are suitable for Primary children and the teacher uses them to help the children gain information, to find answers to questions, to add to enjoyment, and to interpret life, they will often furnish a more effective use of literature for religious guidance than storytelling. Primary children are learning to read. "Let me read for myself," Charles said one day. "Don't tell me stories. I can read fast." And he could.

Books that are used for this purpose should usually grade one grade lower than the readers that the children use at school. Reading for enjoyment and to carry out projects should be largely free and without difficulty. The books should be on various levels of ability, from simple picture books to third-grade books for the advanced readers. Some of the books the children may make themselves out of their folders and out of stories in their story papers.

The children's folders in our more advanced graded courses can be bound together in the form of readers. One of the most satisfying experiences of a first- and second-grade group was making such a book from the folders that are part of a unit entitled "Children of the Bible."

How does the teacher help the children to use the book table or corner? The shortness of time is a real limitation, for children must linger over books and come slowly to see them as sources of ideas and information. Some ways to stimulate its use at church school are: Direct the children to it on arrival; make a list of children who are to look up certain information or a poem or a picture or a song for the group. The place in the book should be marked. Send the children to books to find answers to questions that arise in a discussion. Get the children to look for poems or prayers to use in working out a program.

When these plans are used, children often bring books for the table. One discussion of the solar system in a third grade brought four books the next Sunday.

Referring to something found in a book in conference time or letting children show pictures that they have found helps to keep the children interested in using the book table.

The child's story. The first and second grades like to make story charts of their own group life. These are recorded on large pieces of paper or cardboard. The children dictate the story. The teacher records it with black crayon or with a speed ball pen and India ink. Then the children read it over and over. These large sheets may be bound in a book. It makes a splendid record of the year's work and stimulates further planning. One third grade made and illustrated one entitled "Outdoor Life in Palestine." Sometimes the second or third grade will enjoy making a book of riddles and illustrating it. It may be about helpers, other children, friendly people, workers.

The Bible story book. The Bible story book may have a place on the reading table. There is no dearth of Bible story books; but suitable ones are like wells in a desert, few and far between. One of the real needs of religious education today is a series of beautifully and suitably illustrated Bible readers. The selection of materials will be in keeping with the needs, abilities, and maturity of Primary children. They will be written for the children to read.

Only a beginning has been made in furnishing suitable Bible story books for Primary children. One group of Primary teachers collected the Bible story books in their community book stores. They secured and evaluated fifty different books. They rejected any books that used Bible stories like the Flood, the stories of Moses, Daniel in the lion's den, because they considered these stories too mature for Primary children. Any books with presentation in pictures of the mystical side of religion were ruled out as likely to confuse children. Any books that followed a chronological arrangement were considered unsuitable. The books chosen are listed on pages 101-2.

The religious books that talk down to children and describe an artificial religious experience, like many of the interpretations of the Lord's Prayer, are a hindrance to their normal religious growth. Any trivial organizations of biblical material miss the point.

Primary and Junior children need a children's Bible. It is hoped that one may be prepared. In the meantime an old family Bible with its large type is a good addition to the Primary reading table. Along with it the teacher should have a copy of a modern translation so that she and her children can read with both the spirit and the understanding.

Memorization. Memorizing Bible verses, poems, and songs may be considered a use of literature with children. It should be planned to carry out the following purposes: to give the children beautiful word forms in which to express themselves and to give them clearer ideas of Christian teaching that they may follow in daily living. The children should always have a reason for memorizing the passage. Often they may make it their own responsibility to learn it. One first- and second-grade group used many lovely devotional verses from the Bible, a springtime hymn, and a prayer set to music to make a worship service for Easter. The children drilled each other until they mastered the materials. I have seen little groups of children in a vacation school helping each other to learn verses which they had decided they needed.

Children learn well if the amount of material for memorization is limited and adjusted to the length of session. There should be many opportunities to recall and use memory materials over and over again. Then they are really learned. Of course no Primary child can be expected to learn a verse in a session. Children do not memorize so rapidly.

Often one important Bible verse can be chosen and used during the teaching of a unit. It will be associated with many experiences and used in many ways. Sometimes older Primary children will take a longer passage, like Psalm 100, and use it during several weeks.

Primary children should have a chance to choose the verses that they memorize from among those furnished in the course of study. More are always suggested than any one child can learn. Religious inspiration comes to individuals from different materials. The Bible verse that means much to one person has little meaning for another. This individual difference is just as true of children.

Some Primary teachers make booklets of all the Bible verses for a unit and place it on the reading table. Other teachers make large charts of verses the children have chosen and hang them on the wall.

There will always be some children in a Primary group who do not profit religiously by memorizing verses, poems, and hymns. They should not be expected to do so. What helps one child at a certain time has no motivating power for another. The teacher should know each child so well that she can help him to grow religiously through the methods to which he responds.

FOR FURTHER STUDY

Barnes, Walter. *The Children's Poets.* New York: World Book Co., 1924.

Dalgliesh, Alice. *First Experiences with Literature.* New York: Charles Scribner's Sons, 1937. Chaps. I, III, VI.

500 Books for Children. Washington: Superintendent of Documents.

(This graded list reflects the judgment of many elementary workers. Price, 15 cents.)

Gardner, Emelyn E., and Ramsay, Eloise. *A Handbook of Children's Literature.* Chicago: Scott, Foresman & Co., 1927. Chaps. I-III, IX.

Hazard, Paul. *Books, Children and Men.* The Horn Book. Boston, 1944.

MacClintock, Lander. *Literature in the Elementary School.* Chicago: University of Chicago Press, 1907.

Minor, Ruby. *Early Childhood Education.* New York: D. Appleton-Century Co., 1937. Chap. XIV.

Mitchell, Lucy Sprague. *Here and Now Story Book.* New York: E. P. Dutton & Co., 1921. Introduction.

Sawyer, Ruth. *The Way of the Storyteller.* New York: The Viking Press, 1942.

Seeling, Martha, chairman. *A Bibliography of Books for Young Children.* Washington: Association for Childhood Education, 1939. (Bulletin.)

Smither, Ethel L. *The Use of the Bible with Children.* New York: Abingdon-Cokesbury Press, 1937. Chaps. I-III, VII.

Stolper, J. B. *The Bulletin Board as a Teaching Device.* New York: Bureau of Publications, Teachers College, Columbia, University.

Stories Children Like. Washington: Association for Childhood Education.

Storm, Grace E., and Smith, Nila B. *Reading Activities in the Primary Grades.* Boston: Ginn & Co., 1930. Chaps. VII, VIII.

Storytelling. Washington: Association for Childhood Education, 1941.

BOOKS FOR THE PRIMARY CHILDREN
Poetry

Association for Childhood Education, compilers. *Sung Under the Silver Umbrella.* New York: The Macmillan Co., 1935.

Barrows, Marjorie, compiler. *Two Hundred Best Poems for Boys and Girls.* Racine, Wis.: Whitman Publishing Co., 1938. (Price, 10c.)

Diamond, Lucy. *When He Was Just a Little Child.* London: Oxford University Press, 1940. (Out of print but unusually helpful. Your library may have it.)

Harrington, Mildred P., compiler. *Ring-A-Round.* New York: The Macmillan Co., 1930.

Rossetti, Christina G. *Sing Song.* New York: The Macmillan Co., 1912.

Thompson, Blanche J., compiler. *More Silver Pennies.* New York: The Macmillan Co., 1938.

——— *Silver Pennies.* New York: The Macmillan Co., 1925.

Nature

Beauchamp, W. L., and others. *Science Stories, Books I and II.* Chicago: Reilly & Lee Co., 1934.

Bourgeois, Florence. *Beachcomber Bobbie.* New York: Doubleday, Doran & Co., 1935.

Brown, Margaret Wise. *Night and Day.* New York: Harper & Bros., 1942.

Buckley, H. M., and others. *Around the Year.* New York: American Book Co., 1942.

Buff, M. M. and C. *Dash & Dart.* New York: The Viking Press, 1942.

Craig, G. S., and Burke, Agnes. *We Find Out.* Boston: Ginn & Co., 1940.

Frasier, G. W., and others. *Sunshine and Rain.* Syracuse, N. Y.: L. W. Singer Co., 1938.

O'Donnell, Mabel, and Carey, A. E. *Round About.* Evanston: Row, Peterson & Co., 1941. (See "The Blue Pool.")

Parker, Bertha M. *Living Things.* Evanston: Row, Peterson & Co., 1941.

Patch, Edith M. *First Lessons in Nature Study.* New York: The Macmillan Co., 1926.

Robin Sings, The. (Unit Activity Reader.)

Wavle, Witty, and Falk. *Rain and Shine.* Boston: D. C. Health Co., 1942.

Woodpecker Taps, The. (Unit Activity Reader.)

Friendliness

Freivogel, Esther. *All Around the City.* New York: Friendship Press, 1938.

Prayers

Burdekin, Harold. *A Child's Grace.* New York: E. P. Dutton & Co., 1938.

Jones, Mary Alice, editor. *My Own Book of Prayers.* Chicago: Rand McNally & Co., 1938.

——— *Prayers for Little Children.* Chicago: Rand McNally & Co., 1937.

Simpson, N., and Cox., L. E. *Children's Praises.* London: Student Christian Movement Press, 1934.

Bible Books for Small People

Entwistle, Mary. *Isaac of the Tents.* New York: Thomas Nelson & Sons, 1935.

——— *When Jesus Was a Boy.* New York: Thomas Nelson & Sons, 1932.

Jones, Jesse and Jones, Elizabeth Orton. *Small Rain.* New York: The Viking Press, 1943.

For the Reading Table

Lobingier, Elizabeth M. *Hebrews Home Life.* Chicago: University of Chicago Press, 1926. (For third grade only.)

Moore, Jessie Eleanor. *Bible Stories to Read.* New York: Thomas Nelson & Sons, 1930.
------ *First Bible Stories.* New York: Thomas Nelson & Sons, 1929.
Petersham, Maud and Miska. *The Christ Child.* New York: Doubleday, Doran & Co., 1931. (For third grade only.)
------ *Ruth.* Philadelphia: The John C. Winston Co., 1938.
Pewtress, Vera. *Our Church: the House of Praising.* London: Student Christian Movement Press, 1939.
Smither, Ethel L. *Jesus and the Children.* New York: Thomas Nelson & Sons, 1929.

For First and Second Grade

Beskow, Elsa. *Pelle's New Suit.* New York: The Platt & Munk Co., 1930.
Gates, Huber and Peardon. *Jim and Judy.* New York: The Macmillan Co., 1939.
Gay, Witty, and Wright. *A Home for Sandy.* Boston: D. C. Heath Co., 1942.
Hader, Berta H. and Elmer. *The Little Town.* New York: The Macmillan Co., 1941.
Hanna, P. R., and Anderson, Genevieve. *Peter's Family.* Chicago: Scott, Foresman & Co., 1935.
Lindman, Maj Jan. *Snipp, Snapp, Snurr and the Red Shoes.* Chicago: Albert Whitman & Co., 1932. (And other books of this author.)
Sharpe, Stella Gentry, *Tobe.* Chapel Hill, N. C.: University of North Carolina Press, 1939.
Stanger, Margaret A. *A Brand New Baby.* Boston: The Beacon Press, 1942.

For Third Grade

Bannon, Laura. *Manuela's Birthday in Old Mexico.* Chicago: Albert Whitman & Co., 1939.
Brandt, Rose. *The Colored Land.* New York: Charles Scribner's Sons, 1937.
Burton, Virginia Lee. *Little House.* Boston: Houghton Mifflin Co., 1942.
Clark, Ann. *Little Herder in Autumn* (1940), *Little Herder in Winter* (1942), *Little Herder in Spring* (1940), *Little Herder in Summer* (1942). Phoenix: United States Office of Indian Affairs.
Clark, Ann Nolan. *In My Mother's House.* New York: The Viking Press, 1941.
Credle, Ellis, *Down Down the Mountain.* New York: Cadmus Books, 1940.
Davis, Lavinia. *We All Go Away.* New York: Charles Scribner's Sons, 1940.
------ *We All Go to School.* New York: Charles Scribner's Sons, 1941.

Gay, Zhenya and Jan. *Pancho and His Burro,* New York: William Morrow & Co., 1930.

Hader, Berta H. and Elmer. *The Little Town.* New York: The Macmillan Co., 1941.

—— *Midget and Bridget.* New York: The MacMillan Co., 1934.

Hanna, P. R. and others. *Susan's Neighbors at Work.* Chicago: Scott, Foresman & Co., 1937.

Keiser, Armilda B., *Come Everyone and Worship.* New York: Friendship Press, 1941.

Machetanz, Frederick. *On Arctic Ice.* New York: Charles Scribner's Sons, 1940.

—— *Panuck, Eskimo Sled Dog.* New York: Charles Scribner's Sons, 1939.

Millen, Nina. *A Sari for Sita.* New York: Friendship Press, 1938.

Moore, Jessie Eleanor. *Welcome House.* New York: Friendship Press, 1939.

—— *A Bell for Baby Brother.* New York: Friendship Press, 1944.

Morrow, Elizabeth R. *The Painted Pig.* New York: Alfred A. Knopf, Inc., 1930.

O'Donnell, Mabel, and Carey, A. E. *Friendly Village.* Evanston: Row, Peterson & Co., 1941. (See "The Courage of Singing Boy" and "Feast of Thanksgiving.")

Pease, Josephine V. *We Love America.* Chicago: Rand McNally & Co., 1941. (10c book.)

Sawyer, Ruth. *The Least One.* New York: The Viking Press, 1941.

Thomas, Margaret Loring. *The Burro's Moneybag.* New York: Abingdon-Cokesbury Press, 1931.

FOR FURTHER ACTIVITY

1. Make a list of the purposes in religious guidance that literature helps the teacher realize.

2. List purposes of the next unit in your teacher's book. Go to the children's room at the library or to the nearest public school. Plan to spend at least a morning or an afternoon examining books that can contribute to the achievement of these purposes. Make a list of these books in a notebook. Add a similar list for each unit of the year. You will have a working list of books for your reading table.

3. Find poems that fit in with at least four of the units in the course of study for the year.

4. Sometimes a children's hymn can be used as a poem. Try using one with your group one Sunday this month. Be sure to know how to introduce it. It will be well for you to memorize the poem.

5. Tell what are the limitations of any form of literature in guiding the religious life of children.

Chapter VI

MUSIC EXPERIENCES AND RELIGIOUS GROWTH

Music and religious living. When Primary teachers understand how the power of music causes children to grow, the entire Primary program is full of musical experiences. Music is not set off into a period. It lends meaning to, and heightens the value of, every church experience the children have. Before the regular session begins, the children gather about the pianist to sing some new hymn, to enjoy some familiar ones, or to make their own songs. Some groups sing as they work. A group sings on a trip. And in many other ways music is part of all living and learning at church. This is as it should be, for the church that sings is always a living church. The greatest periods of the history of the church have been the ones when the people sang most gloriously. This is natural, for music added to experience makes life something more than itself.

From the beginning of time life has been more meaningful when celebrated in song. The mighty maker of songs was the first religious leader of his tribe. "How should a man live fully who had no song to sing with his fellows, stamping, grunting, acting the tale which it told? How should the hunt keep the full flavour of its virtue if there were no song afterwards in which to relive its great moments? In the corroboree a man felt himself exalted and renewed; . . . and in remembering a tale and telling it to his children he touched the fringe of immortality." [1]

The teachers of young children, along with all the other leaders of the church, bear responsibility for developing a

[1] Eleanor Dark, *The Timeless Land,* The Macmillan Co., 1941, p. 12.

103

fellowship that knows, enjoys, and worships through great church music.

How music fosters religious growth. Music may contribute to the social and religious growth of children in a number of ways. Music helps children to know the teachings of the Christian church, and leads them to accept these values for their own lives and to build their lives around them.

Many children suffer from emotional tensions that hinder the growth of Christian personality. Music helps to release them from this inner stress and leaves them more at peace with themselves and their associates. Every Primary teacher knows the power of music in re-creating tired, cross children. A vacation church school opened on the day after Independence Day. Only music helped the children to live happily together that day. Children are keenly conscious of rhythm. Their living together at church is helped or hindered by the music that is used.

Primary teachers hope to have a sense of fellowship develop among the children. Music is one source of this "togetherness," for it leads to a sense of common joy. As children sing together, the sense of belonging together develops. As we shall see in Chapter X, this group feeling is an essential of worship.

Music may also create new interests. Sometimes a unit is introduced through the singing or the teaching of a song. Sometimes a new plan grows out of some hymn or song that the children learn.

Music may help a group to enjoy each other and to have genuine fun together. This use of songs is of especial value in vacation church schools and expanded sessions.

The religious heritage of the race may be shared through music. Some of the greatest music of the world is religious in character. Excerpts can be carefully chosen from it and shared with Primary children, especially with the third grade. Not only is a mood stimulated that leads to worship, but listening to the music itself becomes an act of worship. A brief except from the choral in Beethoven's *Ninth Sym-*

phony was used with one group of eight-year-old children with these results.

A good way to introduce Bible verses is to set them to music and use them in meeting the children's need for a fine medium of expression in times of wonder and of sudden insight into the meaning of life or the character of God. "I will sing to the Lord as long as I live" and "The earth is full of the loving-kindness of the Lord" have been used by many Primary children in just these ways. Children are perhaps more closely in tune with the spirit of the Bible when they use its devotional passages as songs than at any other time. "No culture can be completely understood without interpreting its music." [2] We have sometimes forgotten in the teaching of the Bible that it is filled with poetry and music.

Types of music. What kind of music should the church use with Primary children? Most of the music for Primary children will be songs. They should be chosen according to the highest standards of children's music. First of all, the poetry should be good lyric poetry. The expression should be simple, brief, and truly poetic. There should be no talking down to children, as in songs about "little children" or such a self-conscious song as "The Wise May Bring Their Learning." This is an example of the way adults with no understanding of children think they feel. Children at their best do not. No confusing symbolic teaching, as in such a song as "God, Make My Life a Little Light" will be included.

Prayer songs should be addressed to God in order to avoid confusion of the ideas of God and Jesus. The ideas of God that are reflected in the songs should be of a loving Father. He is good. He is the Creator of all the universe. He is the Father of all children.

Songs that refer to God as in heaven, looking down, or of children as looking up only confuse children and keep them in the stage of their first crude ideas of God. One group of Primary teachers who studied the words of every song most carefully wished to use "Do You Know How Many Stars" [3]

[2] *Music Education in the Elementary School,* p. 3, State Board of Education, Sacramento, Calif.
[3] Ida F. Leyda, ed., *Carols,* Leyda Publishing Co.

in a unit on Mexico because this song is sung in Spanish in church schools in Mexico. They studied the song and found that the last line read, "God in heaven knows them all." This line was changed to "God, our Father, knows them all" because the teachers were sure that Primary children were not helped to know God by the original wording. Of course, the words of songs should not be changed unless there is a real reason. If a change is necessary it is usually better not to use the song.

The poetry should use vivid word pictures with a strong appeal to the senses and should lift the experiences of life to a high level of appreciation. Abstract words and conventional religious terms should be avoided. A Primary child is having the experiences that will later lend meaning to these terms.

The pianist should be a sensitive musician who knows how to play for children—simply, without runs or trills, and with the melody accented. The music should be played in the same octave in which the children sing. She works with all the teachers on the music in the course of study. Children must sing a song in many different situations and many times before they really know it. For this reason, primary teachers use those songs that can become part of many units of experience and sing them with new meaning throughout the year. Of course, this means not using the same song Sunday after Sunday but joyful re-use of meaningful songs. Most of the Primary courses of study suggest this use of music for children.

Many experts in children's music think that children should learn new songs without piano accompaniment at first. If the teacher is not sure of the trueness of pitch of her voice, she may purchase a pitch pipe and ask a musician to show her how to use it.

When to use music. Some ways in which music may enter into the experience of Primary children may be reviewed. Music should be taught at that point in the living of the group when the desire to sing is at its highest. Teachers cannot wait for a music-teaching time or a "worship service" to introduce all songs; for then the moment will be lost, never to be regained. The m .sic that accompanies a course of study is an essential part of it. It is intended for use in both large group and class. In fact there is real value in small-group singing during the class or group tim · for it gets many children to take part who would not sing at first in the large group. There is no real distraction as a result of the quiet singing by a group in a Primary room. If the rest of the groups are engaged in purposeful activity, they either do not notice or they join spontaneously in the song.

A song can express the very core of meaning of a unit of experience. One Primary group used the song "God Gives the Year" in this way. Out of its singing grew a frieze of the seasons, search for Bible verses to match the experience of each one, stories that lent meaning to the entire experience, a worship service that was shared with the inmates of a home for the aged at Easter. The service was built around the song. The class spent six weeks on this plan.

Sometimes a song may initiate a unit, both mood and plan. "Silent Night" leads as naturally as breathing into Christmas plans. "The Glad Time" [4] was the motivating song for one Primary group at Christmas. They wanted to make the last line, "And all the world seems kinder," come true.

Songs may express in words the feeling that grows out of experience. A group of children pack a box for a migrant center. They have many learning experiences in connection with the activity. As they watch one of the fathers print the label on the box, they sing, "Friends of All." [5] The naming of experience in the song gives children a fuller understanding of it.

A group of children have grown to appreciate the security that the community workers bring to their lives. They have sensed how this care is part of the loving-kindness of the Lord; so they are stating their trust and expressing their emotional reaction when they sing, "The Earth Is Full of the Loving-kindness of the Lord."

[4] E. L. Thomas, *Sing, Children, Sing,* Abingdon-Cokesbury Press, 1939.
[5] No. 84 in E. L. Thomas, *Sing, Children, Sing,* Abingdon-Cokesbury Press, 1939.

A song can help in the development of group plans. One group worked on plans that led to a religious interpretation of fundamental human needs and provision for them—food, health, clothing, shelter, friends. It centered about the verse, "Your Father knows well that you need them." The hymn "The Song of the Bread" was introduced. In the midst of learning it, a box containing a sheaf of wheat was received from a friend. One boy suggested that they make an illustrated chart with "real things, not just pictures" on it. Later the children were planning to send sun suits to a day nursery as a way of sharing clothing because God intended for all children to have clothing. The children at the day nursery lacked it. Then the group felt the need of a new stanza to the song. This is what they wrote and illustrated:

> Clothes from cloth,
> Cloth from loom,
> All from pretty cotton bloom.
> God with tender, loving care
> Sends clothes to children everywhere.

Songs are sometimes a more natural method of worship than prayer or the recall of Bible verses for young children. Any teacher who has seen her children in a time of great joy singing wholeheartedly "I Will Sing to the Lord" knows the reality of this use of song.

Songs help to lend the dignity and worth to the church experience that the eight-year-old seeks. Such a song as "The Church," certain stanzas of "For the Beauty of the Earth," and "Tell Me the Stories of Jesus" are first hymns for these older Primary children. Of course, as in the case of the younger children, the teacher makes sure that understanding of ideas goes with the singing. She does not take for granted that the words are comprehended by the children.

Songs should be used, as has been said, whenever and wherever they have religious value. The children walk in their beloved little lane one Sunday. They find the forsythias a golden glory. They break into song, "Thank You, God, for the Beautiful World."

The third grade is dramatizing a Bible story. As they paint the background, work on costumes, and choose characters and dialogue, they sing "For Stories Fine and True." [6]

A first grade is setting up a scene. There is a house for a family. In the yard there is a fish pond, a nest in a tree, a house for the dog. As they work they sing "The Home God Gave to Me."

Christmas is here. The children have set up a simple crèche. Now some of them move the figures around to play the story. They sing softly "Silent Night." A group who are wrapping packages for Santa Claus's chimney takes it up. Then the group who are making Christmas gifts for parents joins in. The entire group are singing, and there is a moment of genuine worship.

All of these incidents happened in Sunday sessions of an hour.

The third grade often dramatizes a song. "Bring a Torch, Jeannette, Isabella" is an excellent Christmas carol for dramatization.

Sometimes a song tells a story better than it could be told in prose. "In Little Bethlehem" and "Tell Me the Stories of Jesus" are examples.

Teaching songs. The song should first of all be a part of experience. There should be a motive for learning it. Then the rote method may be used. The first step is listening while leader or pianist sings the song. Then the children may be helped to feel the beat of the song. Then the leader may sing the song again. On the third singing the children may sing the easy phrases, then all of the song. Then they may sing it with the piano. Of course, simple songs need no such teaching. The group sings after hearing the teacher sing once.

Times of listening. Teachers of Primary children are just beginning to give children experiences in listening to music in the church school. One vacation-school group heard an excerpt of "He Shall Feed His Flock," from Handel's *Messiah*. "Just listen again," the leader suggested. Then she

[6] No. 107 in *Sing, Children, Sing*.

asked: "If you were to tell your mother about it, what kind of music would you say it was?"

"Nice and gentle."

"For a baby."

"It's like this," said one boy; and he sang the first two measures.

"Like 'Away in a Manger,'" said a little girl; and, singing the first measures of that carol, she demonstrated how alike in quality and tempo the two were.

The leader said that the music was about how a shepherd took care of his sheep. She told about Oriental shepherds and their tender care for their flocks. Then the pianist played the excerpt again. Her skill in interpretation greatly added to the experience. If the pianist had not been able to play well, a victrola record would have been preferable. A teacher who plays the violin well might have played the excerpt on a muted instrument. This experience occurred in a unit on "Bible Homes and Homes Today" with third- and fourth-grade children. It lent enrichment to this study.

At a special festival time music can give the proper mood for the festival and can help the children to avoid overexcitement. Chopin's Opus 28, No. 20, and Handel's "The Joyous Farmer" are good Thanksgiving selections. At Christmas the leader may use Handel's "He Shall Feed His Flocks," Brahms's "Lullaby," and any of the Christmas carols.

In the springtime, selections from Beethoven's *Sixth Symphony,* the Mozart music that is set to the song "See Now the Laughing Springtime," [7] and the Haydn music for "Lady Daffydowndilly" [8] may be used. Shindig's "Rustle of Spring" is excellent.

In the summer the teacher may use some of MacDowell's music. Selections from Mendelssohn's "Fingal's Cave" and Schubert's "The Sea" are good.

Music can help children to have brief times of quietness. This aspect of its use will be dealt with more fully in Chapter X.

[7] McConathy, *The Music Hour* (Elementary Teachers Book), Silver Burdett Co.

[8] *Sing, Children, Sing.*

When children create music. When they have the leadership of musical adults, children create music normally and freely. Their leaders show that they anticipate music from the children. Sometimes a song almost sings itself. When the children were eager to sing

> I was glad when they said unto me,
> Let us go into the house of the Lord,

the leader began to say the verse in as rhythmic a way as possible. She asked where the music should go up and where down. How would the song end if they were to write the music?

"Like this," said one child, and sang the phrase. The pianist played it.

"I think it is like this," said a boy slowly. The pianist played his phrase. The group chose. Soon the music for the entire verse was written.

Sometimes children ask teachers to make songs for them. One day after the session was over, a Primary teacher and a pianist were talking. The pianist played an excerpt from Haydn's *Concerto in G. Major* to illustrate a point.

"I know that," a little boy came running up to them.

A little girl joined them. "We heard it at school. Papa Haydn wrote it."

"Write us a song to go with it," the boy asked the leader.

"Don't you like it just as it is?" she asked.

"No, I want a song."

"One has already been written to this music," said the leader; and she sang "Lovely Spring Has Come Again." [9]

"That's not what I want, and I want you to make a song," the boy insisted.

"What shall it be about?" the teacher asked.

"About a baby," he answered.

"Your little new brother. A gay, happy song because you are so happy to have him?"

The boy nodded. He was relaxed now, for he was under-

[9] *Songs for Little Children*, United Church of Canada, The Ryerson Press.

stood. So the teacher wrote and the group sang gaily and gladly:

> Father God, for all thy joys
> Thanks we sing so freely,
> But our happiest thanks of all
> For a little baby.

The song swept the group into some of the most meaningful work of the year as they expressed friendliness and care for tiny children in home, church, and community agencies.

The writing of an operetta is reported on page 156.

The music of the church. When an important music occasion is to take place at the church, the leader should help the children to prepare for it and should later enjoy it in retrospect with them. Haydn's *The Creation* was to be given at a vesper service. The leader talked to the third grade about it. She read them parts of the first chapter of Genesis and of Psalms 104. She told them to listen for certain parts—the birds, the dove cooing, the rolling sea, the tawny lion, the impatient steed, and even the worm. She led them to expect the triumph of the line "And there was light" and the rejoicing of "Achieved is the glorious work." Many of the children were present. They were eager to enjoy excerpts from the oratorio all over again in their own room. The music meant much more to them because of the opportunity.

Sources of songs. The best source of songs is the course of study. These songs are necessary to the successful guidance of learning. Each teacher should make up her own annotated scrapbook of songs. They may be listed by teaching units, festivals of the Christian year, and subjects. Some songs that are valuable ones for Primary children are:

"Tell Me the Stories of Jesus"
"Silent Night," stanza 1.
"Come Softly, Tread Gently." [10]
"In Little Bethlehem"
"In the Early Morning"
"Lord of the Sunlight"
"The Song of the Bread"

[10] There are many translations. The one by Deming is recommended.

"Lovely Spring Has Come Again" (song of the seasons)
"The Church"
"The Father's Care"
"The Child Jesus"
"Friends of All"
"For Stories Fine and True"
"The Home God Gave to Me"
"Blue Sky, Soft and Clear"
"Who Made Earth and Sea and Sky"
"When Each One Has a Secret" or "The Glad Time"
"All Things Bright and Beautiful"
Bible verses set to music.

In summary we may quote: "Music should function in relation to the entire curriculum to which it has a dual function. It may enrich, broaden, and deepen social understanding, but it has a significant contribution to make to human development as an expressive art." [11] And we may add that it is the surest mode of worship for the young child.

FOR FURTHER STUDY

Coleman, Satis N. *Creative Music for Children.* New York: G. P. Putnam's Sons, 1922. (Esp. Chaps. V, VI, VIII.)

Fox, Lillian Mohr, and Hopkins, L. T. *Creative School Music.* New York: Silver, Burdett & Co., 1936.

Gehrkens, Karl Wilson. *Music in the Grade Schools.* Boston: C. C. Birchard & Co., 1934. P. 233.

Krone, Beatrice. *Teaching Music in the Elementary School.* Washington: Progressive Education Association. (Bulletin.)

Lee, J. Murray, and Lee, Doris M. *The Child and His Curriculum.* New York: D. Appleton-Century Co., 1940. Pp. 546-60.

McConathy, Osburne, and Others. *The Music Hour.* New York: Silver, Burdett & Co., 1938.

Music and the Young Child. Washington: Association for Childhood Education, 1926. (Bulletin.)

Music Children Like. Washington: Association for Childhood Education. (Bulletin.)

Music Education in the Elementary School. Sacramento: California State Board of Education, 1940.

*Stinson, E. I.. *How to Teach Children Music.* New York: Harper & Bros., 1941. Chaps. II, III. (A remarkable account of how music released and stabilized handicapped children.)

Thorn, Alice G. *Music for Young Children.* New York: Charles Scribner's Sons, 1929.

[11] *Music Education in the Elementary School.*

Tiegs, Ernest W. *The Management of Learning in the Elementary Schools*. New York: Longsman, Green & Co., 1937. Chap. XI.

Washburne, Carleton W. *A Living Philosophy of Education*. New York: The John Day Co., 1940. Chap. XIII.

*Whipple, Guy M., editor. *Music Education*. Thirty-fifth Yearbook, National Society for the Study of Education, Part II. Bloomington, Ill.: Public School Publishing Co., 1936.

SOME SONGBOOKS

Blashfield, Clara Beers. *Song Friends*. Vaile Co., Rock Island, Ill., 1931.

Coleman, S. N., and Thorn, A. G. *Singing Time*. The John Day Co.

Danielson, F. W., and Conant, G. W. *Song and Play for Children*. Boston: The Pilgrim Press, 1925.

Primary Music and Worship. Westminster Press.

Shields, Elizabeth McE. *Worship and Conduct Songs*. Richmond: Presbyterian Committee of Publications, 1929.

Songs for Little Children. United Church of Canada. The Ryerson Press.

Thomas, Edith Lovell. *Sing, Children, Sing*. New York: Abingdon-Cokesbury Press, 1939.

FOR FURTHER ACTIVITY

1. What is the most important song in the unit you are now teaching? Make a plan to teach it to your class by the rote method as suggested on page —. You may wish to get the aid of the pianist.

2. Select a hymn like "All Things Bright and Beautiful." Illustrate it yourself. Mount your drawings or paintings or the pictures that you find on a long, narrow sheet of wrapping paper. Get a Primary teacher at public school to show you how to write the stanzas in manuscript writing at the top of the paper. How close you will feel to the children when you are done! Now let them make their own illustrations for the hymn. Do not let them see yours until theirs are completed.

3. Choose four songs that express ideas of God. Tell in your own words what these ideas are and why they are Christian concepts. Are they suitable for Primary children? Four good ones to use are "The Father's Care," [12] "All Things Bright and Beautiful," [13] "God Is Near," [14] and "Lord of the Sunlight." [15]

[12] F. W. Danielson and G. W. Conant, *Song and Play for Children*, The Pilgrim Press, 1925.

[13] Found in many hymnals for children.

[14] Elizabeth McE. Shields, *Worship and Conduct Songs*, Presbyterian Committee of Publication, Richmond, Virginia.

[15] F. W. Danielson and G. W. Conant, *Songs for Little People*, The Pilgrim Press, 1905, 1915.

4. Play Brahms's "Lullaby" or the choral from Beethoven's *Ninth Symphony*[16] for the children. Talk with them about the music before you play it. Then ask them to draw pictures to show what the music made them feel.

5. Write in five hundred words an explanation of Primary music at church.

[16] Music of "Joyful, Joyful, We Adore Thee" gives an excerpt that can be used.

Chapter VII

RELIGIOUS GROWTH THROUGH ART EXPERIENCES

Creative experiences. There is no more reason why creative experiences should be discussed in a chapter on growing religiously through art experiences than in any of the other chapters, beginning with Chapter V, of this book. What is a creative experience? To create means to put elements together in new relationships. From the child's point of view, an experience is creative when he arranges elements in ways that are new for him. There can be creative thinking, creative experiences in music, in construction and art, in literature, and in dramatic play. A child sitting back on his heels to gaze at his drawing of a mother bird feeding her young is a creator and knows the joy and the light that never is, on sea or land. What matter if his subject is not an original one? It is new to him, and so it is creative work. He expresses the way an experience has made him feel. He finds, as he works, power and a sense of being at home in the world.

How creative experiences may be motivated. There seem to be definite steps through which a child passes when he has a genuinely creative experience, whether in story-telling, spontaneous dramatization, writing a poem, painting, drawing, using clay, or making a song. Let us see what they are.

One Primary group had a garden. They planted the bulbs in the fall. There was conversation about the wonder of life hidden in them. There was the use of such a Bible verse as "This is the Lord's doing; it is marvelous in our eyes." There was the use of a poem, "The Little Brown Bulbs." In the springtime there were experiences of wonder as leaf, then blossom, appeared. The flowers were shared. There were prayers of wonder and of praise. Then the children wanted to paint pictures of their garden and write stories of their experiences. They used large sheets of newsprint and tempera paints. These children kept smocks at church so that there would be no trouble over spots on clothing. They painted pictures of the garden and of some of their experiences in sharing the flowers. They made a long and glorious frieze that stretched halfway around the room.

Another group were learning a hymn, "All Things Bright and Beautiful." They associated the word pictures in the hymn with their vacation experiences. Betty thought of the noise of Niagara Falls when the group sang "wonderful." Sue had seen "the purple-headed mountain." All of the children had seen "the river running by." They decided to paint pictures of their vacation times, write stories about them, and sing the hymn. Betty drew Niagara Falls, Sue the Smokies, Billy the "Island Queen" on its way to a pleasure resort. There was one fishing picture, and there were many of picnics. Difficulty of subject is no hindrance in the mind of a Primary child. He is in the dramatic or representative stage in art and has no reservations about exactness. They put their large pictures together to make a book, which they entitled "Vacation Scenes."

Let us look at these two incidents. First of all, there were rich and vivid experiences. Children cannot express themselves creatively if they have nothing to say and if they feel nothing. If the children draw airplanes and automobiles or some other stand-by every time they are given crayons or paints, the Primary teacher may be sure that their life at church school needs the stimulation and richness of fresh interests and activities.

Second, there were many materials that helped to arouse emotion and to lead to insight. Poems, hymns, Bible verses, pictures, conversation, were some of them.

Third, there were materials with which to work so that one might express onself. These were suited to Primary children. There were large pieces of paper and tempera paints. There was a place to work.

Fourth, the teachers did not tell the children what to draw or paint. Each child drew out of his own experience.

These four points seem to be the steps in the creative expression of children. Teachers should provide each one.

Working with paints and crayon. The illustrations just given show some ways that children can work with paints and crayons. Paints are a better form of expression for children because they can get better effects with freer movements of the large muscles. On the other hand, the teacher has to plan carefully to keep both room and children from becoming too messy. The children paint with large brushes on large sheets of paper. Small work requires a use of muscle coordinations in hand and eye that Primary children do not yet have. Newspapers should be spread out under the paintings. Water in jars should be at hand. In some classes there may be easels, and a few children can paint at them while others do different work. Sometimes the children can paint on paper attached to the wall.

Younger Primary children are not so likely to paint large friezes or murals that require much advanced planning. They think as they paint. Older seven-year-olds and eight-year-olds can do splendid large pictures that are painted co-operatively. Each section is blocked out, or the entire picture is sketched with chalk. Then the children work by sections or take turns painting. Since they have all planned the picture, each one may work on it. Large pictures of the seasons may be created in this way.

Four girls made a large painting of choir girls singing carols one Christmas. They chose parts to work on after one child had sketched it at the others' direction. The four thought through the picture together.

In the same way three boys made a large painting of the Wise Men coming to Bethlehem.

Big, important work that takes all the free time for several sessions is valuable; for it gives the children an interest that carries over from week to week and helps them to create something of which they are justly proud. It also leads them to think carefully as they create.

Primary children like to use enamellac and lacquer paints also. Out of cheese boxes they can make doll beds or blocks or trains for the nursery class or for a church center. They delight to paint them. Often, dressed in smocks, they work on old newspapers spread out on the floor. One Primary group included among its rules, "No smock, no painting." Some teachers may wish to use this work only in vacation or weekday session. The workers and church must decide.

Crayons may be used to create some object or background that the children need to carry out a plan. They may, for example, sketch the stones for the wall of a Palestinian house that they have made or color cloth for an Egyptian collar needed for a play. They may also express feelings and ideas with crayons, though this is not so natural a medium for younger children as painting.

Every Primary room should have a supply table where the children who act as a committee to assist the supply secretary place what the department needs for work on that morning. This plan saves time for the teachers. It also suggests interesting activity to children.

Often the teacher can tell through the pictures that a child draws when he has gained confused or inaccurate ideas from an experience and can see that it is repeated and that he is given guidance in keener observation. She can also discover fear, loneliness, or some other emotional need in a child's picture. Unless adults find out what children really learn from what goes on, they cannot check on the effectiveness of their teaching. Often free work with paints or crayons will help a handicapped child to find himself by forgetting himself.

Pictures. Enjoying pictures can be a creative experience also. Children in the Primary group can learn from pictures in at least three ways:

First, there are the permanent pictures that help to provide the atmosphere of the room. They will be few in number. They will be of a type that brings an emotional reaction in addition to the information they may give. From time to time they may be changed because of their peculiar contribution to forming healthy attitude in connection with some unit of guided experience. Sometimes they will be changed to help the children appreciate the joys of the season. A lovely Madonna and child is more valuable if it is hung just for the Christmas season than if it is a permanent fixture. One Primary teacher uses "Lo, Children Are a Heritage of the Lord" in connection with units on home life. An excellent copy of "Jesus and the Children" makes a good permanent picture. Of course, all pictures should be hung low so that the child can see them without tilting his head to an impossible angle. Pictures hung above a bulletin board or blackboard might just as well be taken down.

The second value of pictures is that they suggest activities. One Primary leader had just assumed responsibility for her group. The children seemed to have the idea that their responsibility was to sit and "behave." The teacher introduced into the room pictures of Primary children active at church. She called attention to the pictures, and soon her group were busily at work. They had good ideas and no longer came in just to sit and wait for a service to begin.

Third, pictures are invaluable in giving information and recording discoveries. Each Primary group should have sets of charts that have a picture with a word or a sentence or two below it. These pictures may be filed by subjects—helpers, foods, Bible customs, ways children live, and so on. The children may consult them instead of depending on the teacher for information.

There are certain standards to observe in choosing pictures for Primary children. First, there are Bible pictures. These should be simple of detail. Too many historical elements are confusing to children. If possible, they should give an authentic Palestinian setting so that the child sees the event against correct background and customs.

Bible pictures for Primary children should be objective, not subjective and mystical in treatment. Pictures of angels, halos, heavenly light, the presence of the Risen Christ, are highly confusing to children when they are still literalists. Such pictures cause them to associate religion with magic in

an unfortunate way. Many Bible-story books have such unsuitable illustrations. Also, some Primary leaders think that
pictures like the Margaret Tarrant "The Dayspring from on
High" and "The Star of Bethlehem" have more of confusion
than of value for Primary children.

There should be other pictures for Primary children to
enjoy and use. Some valuable pictures are seasonal pictures;
pictures of animals, birds, butterflies, moths; activity pictures; and pictures of children.

Teachers should be sure that the child understands the
details of the picture and does not interpret them in ideas
that have no connection with the picture. Often children
think men with beards in Bible pictures are Santa Claus. Who
else in their environment is so adorned?

Pictures should be kept in files. If a regular file is not
available, one can be made in a large cardboard carton, or
several of them can be used for different kinds of pictures.

Clay. Clay is another medium of expression for Primary
children. At first they are likely just to squeeze it and manipulate it in other ways. This seems to be a necessary first stage
in the use of any material by children, and some Primary
children still manipulate any art medium at first. Soon they
use it to carry out their ideas. They may model the household
articles for an Oriental peep show or the *casuelas* for a
Mexican kitchen. They may grow to respect Indian art when
they try to model and decorate pottery with Indian designs.
Younger Primary children may make bowls for their mothers
at Mother's Day. They paint them with gay colors and shellac
them. Of course, not even the third grade is ready to work
with the coil. All Primary children should work from the
lump.

A small covered garbage can or a large stone jar is an
excellent container for clay, especially if a damp cloth is
placed around the clay and folded over the top.

The teacher can buy clay powder in five-pound packages.
She should mix it with water to a stiff dough consistency
about twenty-four hours ahead of the time for its use. Then

the mass can be wrapped in a damp cloth. Each child should have a piece as large as he can hold in his two hands.

When the children are working, water in a pan should be available to wet drying clay. When the clay is modeled, it should be set in a safe place to dry. At another session it may be painted. Sometimes children model small objects. At other times they make life-size ones. Sue and Tim modeled an Oriental lamp for the large Oriental house. They painted and shellacked it, plaited a wick, and burned olive oil in it to make a light. Some teachers keep old pieces of oilcloth to cover the tables during clay work. Newspapers should be spread on the floor around the tables.

Wood. Primary children, especially in vacation school, need wood to work with. The report of the little cart, page 47, that was made from a grape box, old wheels, and a broomstick is one example of how children with a little help may make really worth-while articles. Making blocks and beds has been discussed. Very nice doll beds and real child chairs may be made of apple boxes. Orange crates make bookcases and doll houses. Wood salvaged from boxes makes chests. The resourceful Primary teacher will collect and keep all sorts of "waste" materials and encourage parents and children to do likewise.

The Primary room in many a small, poorly equipped church became a real children's room by the use of an orange-crate bookcase. Then a kitchen table had legs sawed off to make a children's work table. Both pieces of equipment were painted. Then inexpensive toys were made, pictures collected and filed in a paper carton, and a few good inexpensive books secured. Parents, teachers, and children worked together to make a real place of learning for the children.

Whenever possible, the children should engage in large enterprises that extend over a period of several weeks. One Primary group, with the sexton's help, built an Oriental house out of three grand piano boxes. It was a cube 6 feet long by 5 feet wide by 6 feet high. There was an outside stairway, a balustrade around the roof, a door, a tiny latticed window.

The children made a large Oriental lamp out of clay, painted and shellacked it, and placed it on a shelf inside. It really burned oil and made a light. They covered the house with gray paper on which they had made "stones" with black crayon. The walls inside were hung with bright rugs that the children painted on large sheets of wrapping paper. This work took weeks. It required much research into what homes were like in Bible times. The house lent itself to dramatic play, to the asking of many questions, to times of worship. Somehow, it seemed easy really to ask about the things that puzzled you when you sat on the floor in your house and imagined you lived there long ago and wondered about things.

The house meant so much to the children that they refused to dismantle it. To the leader's surprise, succeeding groups refurnished it joyfully. Some of the group that built it, even when they were in Junior High, would drift in every now and then. "Miss S ——, may I sit in the house?" The child would disappear inside. As he left the room later, he would smile at the leader.

Another group planned to make a village to show how friendly people lived. It soon became the center for their own neighborhood, a square where the community life centered. It was built of boxes in one corner of the Primary room and on a base of several large pieces of corrugated paper that were fitted together. It grew gradually as the children had contacts with friendly people; church, school, and firehouse were added to the neighborhood.

When Christmas time came, the children centered their Christmas activities about the square. They decorated it for Christmas just as the real square was decorated; they learned a carol to sing at their square just as they were singing carols in the real square. They put a tree with repaired toys in their friendly town, just as they carried toys to the firehouse on their real square.

Sewing. Primary children, especially the boys, love to sew. The fact that they cannot thread needles easily or sew a fine seam does not deter them in the least.

One group gleefully made the mattresses, sheets, pillows,

and nightgowns for the doll beds for the nursery class. This group was composed of boys, except for one little girl who threaded the needles.

Children can stuff and lace together oilcloth rabbits for younger children. The holes should be punched large enough for the work to go easily.

Cooking. Cooking is an ever-abiding interest of Primary children, and a genuine art expression. Some groups have made apple jelly at Thanksgiving for the inmates of a home for the aged. They stuffed dates with a paste of ground nuts and raisins for Valentines.

They have made orange marmalade or cookies at Christmas time. The cooking group should be kept reasonably small and the recipes reasonably simple. They should be printed on a large chart that the children may consult. Often the children bring the ingredients and grow in a sense of social responsibility as they do so. Most of the cooking is planned on Sunday and done during the week.

Scrapbooks and posters. Younger Primary children do not express themselves well by making scrapbooks, for the teachers have to do too much of the thinking.

Older Primary children can make simple ones like a "Book of My Church" or "Friendly People."

Most posters with many pictures pasted on them are really teacher work. Painting or drawing is a much better expression for children.

Keep activities under control. Teachers wish children to have an active, happy time at church. This is not their only aim, however. The wise teacher sees beyond the activity itself to the religious growth that it should help her to realize for the children. She is careful to think about what they do. She wants them to grow in the ability to live together in brotherly ways at church, to take more responsibility for the church, to express friendliness and responsibility for others in the spirit of the Second Great Commandment, and to learn new insights into the character of God and of their relation to him. So she looks upon the use of activities as her most powerful teaching method. She uses them with a purpose and not just to keep children busy or happily occupied.

To use activities well, the teacher must obey certain rules. First of all, she remembers the length of her session and the time that elapses between sessions and makes her choice of activities on this basis. The three-hour expanded session on Sunday morning or the daily period of the vacation church school offer a splendid environment for important investigations, construction work, committee or individual trips and interviews. These plans must be greatly simplified in the one-hour session on Sunday morning. They can and should be used, however, so the first rule for controlling activities is, Attempt only what the children can accomplish in thoughtful, unhurried fashion and with a real sense of satisfaction.

This rule does not limit the Sunday church school to trivial or useless work. The teachers can use the time to best advantage when they select large activities and work on them session by session instead of doing piecemeal work that can be finished in a short time.

The teacher chooses activities purposefully. As a second rule we may say, Choose activities to accomplish purposes in religious guidance. Activities are worthy of introduction when they help children to live in more social ways, gain insight into religious truth, and participate in a Christian fellowship and worship.

The teacher chooses an activity that is suited to the age of the children. So the third and fourth principles for controlling activities may be stated: The activity must be a large one that can grow gradually as the children build it out of their own learnings. And the activity must be graded to, and challenge, the abilities of the children. Aimless drawings to fill in time and coloring of outline pictures with crayons are, of course, ruled out.

Fifth, many ambitious activities thoughtlessly undertaken and never completed will be avoided. A good teacher is a capable organizer and housekeeper. She sees that what is begun is completed. In order to do this, teachers check themselves week by week to see that the class does not dawdle. Often this means that the teacher keeps herself alert to carry through the activity thoughtfully. She checks the class work after each session to see what ideas are developing, which need introduction, and how to introduce them. She sees that all the materials that will probably be needed for the work of each session are available, that the children's work is put away safely or undisturbed, and that they may pick it up on arrival.

Sixth, the teacher encourages both parents and children to make contributions from home and community life. Parents may drop in to report some friendly happening that has real religious value; the children may bring supplies. One of the fathers may supervise certain work.

Seventh, when an activity is under way the teacher is eager to use the children's reactions in order to make them conscious of any problems that arise, to help them solve these problems, and to try out and weigh their solutions in such a way that new insights and purposes develop. The stories, poems, songs, pictures, and Bible verses that are introduced are used for these purposes. In other words, the materials enrich the activity; not the activity the teaching materials. So we may state our next principle: Teachers use activities to help children think in social and religious fields and, as insights grow, to worship.

Eighth, there is variety in activity to care for special interests and individual differences of the children.

Ninth, the teacher uses the special abilities of the children. Not every child can do the same work well. The teacher helps each one to use what he has and to develop his skill. Charles reads with third-grade ability, so he looks up the information about community helpers in books on the reading table. Nancy and Sue, who are good readers also, work with him. Ralph prints well, so he makes signs. George's father is the fire captain down at the square, so he has first-hand contacts there that the other children do not have. Roger and Buddy love to paint, so they recondition the toys.

Tenth, the teacher keeps the activity under control by helping the children to make a record of it at the end. For example, the children who made the friendly town, see page

49, packed the town away carefully "because we may need it to show later on." They enjoyed in retrospect different parts of the activity and recalled what they had learned about friendly people and about being friendly. They sang "Friends of All" and "The Earth Is Full of the Loving-kindness of the Lord."

Eleventh, as the children were packing, the teacher took one of the little houses in her hand. "I wonder how people live in each one of these little houses," she said. "Do they have good times? Do they help each other? I wonder." "Let's find out," said one child. So the group was launched on a new major investigation and study, to enrich their insights into the values of home life. The teacher found that a good activity, purposefully introduced, developed, and completed, leads on into other worth-while enterprises.

Twelfth, art experiences help some children to trust themselves and others to gain that respect of their own group that is essential to their growth. Philip was a child who expected to fail. One summer he worked in a unit on the "Boyhood of Jesus." He was interested in making one of the chests in which clothes and family treasures were kept. The children had set up a Nazareth carpenter shop. Unfortunately, Philip worked with inferior wood, and the brads tore out each time he put them in. Dejection settled upon the boy. "I knew I could not do it," was written all over him. Then his teacher came to the rescue. "We made a mistake in our wood, Phil," she said. "Let's look at it carefully so we'll know what kind to choose." The two studied the defective wood, chose and tested new pieces. Philip made a splendid chest, and the light of self-esteem shone in his eyes when the head teacher expressed her appreciation of it. "My, but it pays to stick to a job," she said. "You showed me that, Philip."

Then there was Bobby. Bobby was a dull child who never could make the other children admire what he did. And so desperately did he want their respect. Then one day the children were making clay pots to hold pansies for Easter gifts. Bobby shone, for he had a way with clay. "Bobby, how did you get that lovely roundness to your bowl? Do show us," the teacher said. Bobby grew inches in self-respect and happiness at church as the children waited for him to show them how to work. If the Christian religion teaches the supreme worth of every human being, surely this was teaching religion to that Primary group. It was close in spirit to the gospel record.

Our church schools are schools where children learn through practice what it means to live the life of good will and of a trusting child of a Father God. Activity properly controlled is the fundamental method through which their religious growth is guided.

Summary. If children are to grow religiously through art experiences, the following conditions must be cared for:

1. The boys and girls must have rich experiences that lead them to want to express thought and feeling.

2. There must be a variety of materials with which to work.

3. The children should have songs, poems, pictures, and Bible verses and stories. Activity should be the basis of the entire plan. The materials help it along and help to realize religious purpose through it.

4. The teachers should keep hands off. This is no time to tell children what to make. The teacher may be a guide, a consultant, a provider, a stimulator; but she must not do the thinking for the children. One eight-year-old boy was the only child in one Primary group who wanted to paint at first. He was provided with materials. He was exposed to all sorts of experiences. Still he came hopelessly to the teacher.

"Tell me what to paint," he said.

"I couldn't," the teacher replied, "Then I would be painting instead of you. I might give you an idea or two on how to start." She suggested that he look at pictures, watch what the other groups were learning, read the books on the reading table, and just enjoy the use of brush and paints. First the boy painted a Mexican scene that was copied from a book. Then after he read a story, he made an original illustration. The teacher gave him constant encouragement.

"How lovely that red is, George. Why your pictures make me feel Mexican. What a furry-eared little burro!"

She could see by the glint of his eye that her encouragement kept him going on to new ventures. Later he watched a group make panoche, a Mexican candy, and painted a group of Mexican children making it. The stages in his creativeness are quite evident. The teacher learned that he was "taking art lessons" where he was given exact instructions and models. This type of teaching had blocked his creativeness.

5. The work should be big. The children work on large sheets of newsprint, bogus, frieze, or wrapping paper. Primary children do not yet have such muscular co-ordination that they work well in small media, for they have poorly co-ordinated smaller muscles.

6. The activities should be ongoing. Many church schools attempt choppy and unrewarding activities because they have not learned that work can begin where it left off last time and continue until the children complete it. It is hard to complete in one session an activity with religious value.

7. Not all the children should work with the same materials or in the same way. This is the advantage of the grade or double grade, with interest groups, over the class, where usually everyone must do the same thing. Some Primary departments with several classes within the grade have different activities going on in each one. The children choose the activity. If all choose the same one, of course all the classes do the same thing; but this seldom happens.

8. Of course, teachers will not compare one child's work with that of another. If any choice is made of work to be put on the wall or shown, the children make it. The teacher will teach better standards of art by encouraging the good instead of criticizing the poor.

9. Work should be kept and lived with. It is a true record of the children's thinking, feeling, and learning. A frieze of the seasons that extended around two sides of the room was one of the cherished possessions of one group. It was a way of recalling old experiences and also a suggester of new ones. One group made a practice of putting away worth-while work

and of taking it out from time to time for recall, enjoyment. and suggestion.

10. Of course, the teachers will never laugh at any child's drawing. This truly crushes his spirit and fails him religiously. The crude art work of childhood is no funnier to the sympathetic teacher than the sincere expressions of the primitives. Both are pictures of the painter's inner life.

FOR FURTHER STUDY

Cole, Natalie R. *Arts in the Classroom.* New York: The John Day Co., 1940.

Hockett, John A., and Jacobsen, E. W. *Modern Practices in the Elementary School.* Boston: Ginn & Co., 1938. Chap. VI.

Lane, Robert H. *The Teacher in the Modern Elementary School.* Boston: Houghton Mifflin Co., 1941. Chap. IX.

*Lee, J. Murray, and Lee, Doris M. *The Child and His Curriculum.* New York: D. Appleton-Century Co., 1940. Chap. XIV. (Esp. pp. 537-46, 561-68.)

Major, Charlotte R. *Teaching Art in the Elementary School.* New York: Progressive Education Association. (Bulletin.)

Mathias, Margaret E. *The Beginnings of Art in the Public Schools.* New York: Charles Scribner's Sons, 1924.

Minor, Ruby. *Early Childhood Education.* New York: D. Appleton-Century Co., 1937. Chap. XVII.

Mossman, Lois Coffey. *Principles of Teaching and Learning in the Elementary School.* Boston: Houghton Mifflin Co., 1929. Chap. XI.

Use of Waste Materials, The. Washington: Association for Childhood Education. (Bulletin.)

Washburne, Carleton W. *A Living Philosophy of Education.* New York: The John Day Co., 1940. Chap. XII.

FOR FURTHER ACTIVITY

1. List the activities suggested in the unit of work that you are now teaching. Which ones are practical in your situation? Which ones are you using? Try out one that you have never used before. Be sure to get a clear idea of the purpose for its use that is suggested in the teacher's book. Keep a careful record of what you do and what the children do and say as the activity progresses. Through how many class periods does the activity extend?

2. Plan with your superintendent and then carry out an activity that will help the children more fully to realize that God's purposes are back of the universe and its life. Some suggestions are:

Making a seed collection (second and third grade)

Making a weekly chart of time of sunrise and sunset (second and third grades)

Making an investigation to find out how friends of Jesus work (a) to make the community better and safer for all, (b) to show friendliness to some downtrodden group or (c) to some minority group (third grade)

Watching cycle of growth of moth or butterfly (first and second grades)

Watching cycle of growth of chickens or other fowl (first and second grades)

Watching rhythm of seasons and of day and night (all three grades)

4. Suppose a mother visits your class while the children are engaged in some activity that helps them the better to understand God or to live in love and kindness with people. She wonders when you will "teach the children," meaning tell a Bible story. Write in five hundred words how you will explain that the activity is the lesson, the better way to teach young children.

5. Choose two art activities that you have used with Primary children. List what you think the children learned religiously from each one.

6. What handicaps do you face in using activities in your Primary department? Try to work out ways to overcome them. Most of the activities reported in this book were worked out under real handicaps —one-hour sessions and limited equipment.

Chapter VIII

RELIGIOUS GROWTH THROUGH PARTICI-
PATION IN THE PROGRAM OF THE CHURCH

THE religious growth of children is stimulated when their
leaders give them a part in the program of the church. Listen
once more and hear the message of some Primary rooms to
children. Some say: "You come here to listen to a teacher
and a superintendent. There is little for you to do. Unless
you have relationships with the other children outside the
church, you will never make friends here." Other Primary
departments are speaking. They say: "You can live and work
in friendly ways here. You can learn to make friends of
other children. You can learn to know and serve God and
your fellow men. You may have a part in the program of
your church. What you feel, think, and say is of value to
your teachers." The second room is the one that Primary
leaders increasingly are trying to provide for children; for
they see that a child is an apprentice in the Christian religion,
one who learns the way of life as he lives it under the guidance of mature and experienced Christians.

In the Second Great Commandment, Jesus gave a pattern
for the program of activity and fellowship in every Christian
church. Children learn this commandment best when they
have many practical opportunities to make it work in life.
Having teachers explain to them what it means to love one's
neighbor as oneself, hearing stories of people who do love
their neighbors, and singing songs of friendliness—all have a
place in religious teaching. They become important in religious guidance when they lend greater meaning and insight
to the enterprises of good will in which the Primary children
are engaged. Activities that help children to show and feel
love are the real "lessons" through which the teaching of the

Second Great Commandment is realized. Bible verses can make the activity a richer one because they may lead the child into a worship experience in connection with his service. They also give a clearer idea of the religious meaning of his own work.

Primary teachers at church think of ways that the boys and girls can live worthily in the fellowship of the church and take part in the Christian program in the community. They set up certain practical principles to follow in providing an environment of love, friendliness, and service. They want the children to know what "losing one's life" for the welfare of the larger group means. There are many Primary departments where activity of this character goes on all the time. For example, one church was planning its missionary program for the year. Certain tentative plans were outlined. The Primary children were asked to assume certain responsibilities for this program. Leaders studied the plans with their children. The Primary department chose what they would do. Then their choices were approved by the board of education and in turn by the official board of the church.

The Primary children in another church started a plan that spread throughout the church. They wished to send medicine kits to church centers for migrants. The class of young married people to which some of the mothers and fathers belonged became interested and purchased the tin boxes to hold the supplies. A young people's group secured a fine moving picture that showed true conditions among this group of workers. It also showed how church centers served them. The plan enlarged until every group in the church, except the preschool groups, took part in it. One rarely talks with other church-school workers without hearing of such plans.

Fellowship of the group itself. A primary room can be a place where children find friendly adults who care for and have fellowship with each othe . The leaders should know ..ow to work together. This place should give boys and girls chances to make friends under conditions that encourage co-operation. Friendships that exist among the children should be a concern of the teacher. They should be encouraged when they contribute to the development of each child and to the common fellowship. Sometimes these friendships need expansion. Jimmy and Tom were absorbed in each other. They always found something to work on together. They resented the entrance of any other child into this working partnership. This made a problem in the third grade to which they belonged. The leader gradually found activities in which the two boys were interested but which they could not carry out by themselves. She remembered the wise saying of Ortega y Gasset that groups do not come together just to be together, but to do something together. She suggested other children to the two friends, ones who could help them to carry out their purposes. She saw the friendships of both broaden and a greater co-operativeness develop in her class.

Teachers should be friends to individual children also. The child with special need or difficulty or one who comes from a broken home will feel that here at last he has found steady, kindly understanding on which he can depend. Gertrude was an adopted child. The mother was an aggressive person who was often misunderstood and disliked by her neighbors. To retaliate, they spoke disparagingly of the child, never thinking that their own children would heed what they said. The children began to taunt Gertrude at school until the child became so ill she could neither sleep nor eat. Then her mother appealed to the church-school teacher who taught most of the children. She helped the children to see adoption in so favorable a light that any sense of Gertrude's unworthiness was overcome. The group adopted "a little sister" at a children's home. Many of them were "only" children and were happy and excited over the plan. The teacher spoke of how, when we need persons to love and care for, we have a chance to choose them. Then we belong to them, and they to us. She said: "When the home that God has planned to care for a child cannot do it any longer, then it is a part of God's plan for someone else to care. God's plans work in many ways. We can have a part in them." Gertrude grew happier and more expansive at church. She took a passionate interest in the adopted sister, saved her money to help make Christmas for her. The teacher considered that meeting this problem was a challenge and an opportunity to do religious teaching. This is just one of the ways in which the teacher can show children what the Christian life is.

When the Primary department provides an activity program, the relationship of the children to one another is important. This is one of the values of an activity program. The Primary group includes teacher, or guide, as well as children. They live together, work together, talk, share, depend on each other for success of plans, laugh together over some sudden insight, and so learn the interdependence of people. Children must learn this interdependence in the smaller group where emotions are more deeply stirred before they can really care about the fellowships of larger groups.

Primary children need to be trained to seek help from each other, give aid in turn, and appreciate what other children do. Along with this they need to learn to take advice from each other.

The teacher may start by saying: "How nicely Jack read that story. What did you especially like about his reading?"

The children will say: "He read distinctly."

"He understood what he was reading."

"He wanted to read it so that we can go on with our work because he has given us some new ideas."

Then the teacher may say: "Can anyone suggest to Jack some ways to share what he has found in an even more splendid way next time?" Jack is in a softened mood because he is so evidently appreciated and is eager to hear the friendly suggestions of the group. He will learn in time to check on his own work. One brilliant and self-willed little girl literally howled, at first, at what she considered unfriendly advice. In time she said: "I could write this story better. I smeared it. Would you wait with me while I do it over?" Of course the teacher did, and the two proudly posted a very lovely story of Easter time on the bulletin board before they left the church. There is no time in a child's life when he can be trained to take this attitude to group suggestion so well as when he is in the Primary years.

Visitors in the group. The teachers should welcome visitors. Some of these persons will be especially invited to bring information about activities that have been undertaken. The children in one group learn about community helpers. The teacher is leading them to see and feel the interdependence of people. She hopes to have them gradually take a Christian attitude to vocations, to see that one works to serve one's brothers as well as to make a living. The father of one of the boys is a doctor. The children send a committee to invite him to visit them and to help them find out how to keep well. They plan where he is to sit and what questions to ask him. They decide to show him some of their work. The Primary superintendent asks that the visit be shared with the other two grades also. So an activity of a third grade becomes a department plan.

Dr. ——— is greeted at the door by two children and led to his seat. The children sing for him. Then they become too shy to ask their questions; but the leader has made a list of them and, with their evident approval, turns them over to the doctor. One of the teachers, at the suggestion of the leader, makes a record of what the doctor says.

Later the children dictate a letter to thank the doctor for coming. They make a chart of what he told them. They post this chart on the bulletin board, and it is referred to from time to time. When Christmas time comes, they send a greeting to the doctor. "He is one of our friends, you know," one little girl says. All the children sign the card. They have made it by clipping a very lovely Christmas picture from a used Christmas card and mounting it on green construction paper.

Then there are other visitors who come unexpectedly. They may be members of the church who are interested in the children and who like to know what they are doing. These people should be welcomed. They offer an opportunity for the children to have a larger contact with mature Christian personalities than the teachers can give them. "Young children, slow to learn religious creeds, are often quick to detect and

to approve the attitudes of individuals who are truly religious." [1]

Visitors offer a splendid opportunity for the recall and telling of what is going on in the group. Often a child gains a
fuller understanding of an activity when he stops to think
about it and to explain it to another person. One Primary
group adopted a grandmother. None of the children in the
group had a grandmother who lived in the same city. They
had as much need for this contact as did their elderly friend.
She visited them informally and moved from group to group.
The children's faces always brightened when they saw her.
They shared plans and activities with her. Sometimes she
would sit down at a table and work with an interest group.
Sometimes the whole group sang for her. They gave her a
valentine shower on Valentine's Day and always remembered
her birthday.

The "grandmother" went to Florida one winter. When she
came back she brought to the children a carefully selected set
of conch shells graded from the very tiniest specimen to a
huge one. What an enrichment of life for children did this
friendliness bring!

Parents belong where their children are. Sometimes they
become so interested that they greatly enrich the plans of the
group. One summer a Primary group was engaged in enterprises that helped them to realize that God provides the neces-
sities of life—food, clothing, shelter, friends, water. One
mother heard the children sing, "The Song of the Bread."
The next Sunday she brought tiny bread and butter sand-
wiches for every child. "To make the song seem even more
real," she said. Another mother went away to summer camp.
By the next Sunday she sent the children a sheaf of ripe
wheat. A father who kept bees brought a comb of honey.
These parents had made many sensory experiences possible
and so had made the teaching much more vivid.

Children live today in a world where ruthlessness, destruc-
tion, broken faith, and aggressive evil are only too evident.

[1] C. E. Skinner and P. L. Harriman, *Child Psychology*, The Macmillan Co.,
1941, p. 287.

If there was ever a time when teachers needed to remember, "Be not overcome of evil, but overcome evil with good," it is now. These workers can make evident to the children that, even in dark times, denial of Christian teachings and disregard of personality are only a part of life. They can give their children contacts with persons who, by their very lives, say to the boys and girls: "Friendliness, good will, sincerity, and trust in God are realities also. We know that the teachings of Jesus are true. We have lived them. Evil may be abroad in the world, but goodness is still more powerful in influence."

The children gradually learn from their fellowship with Christians that the life of friendliness is more in rhythm with the forces of the universe than fear, hate, or evil; for they are artificial and man-made, not rooted in the character of God. "The power that makes for fellowship is a power not ourselves, with a much longer history than our own and with the marks of belonging to the cosmic process in a much more permanent way than do our frail human bodies. The forces of hate and fear are more nearly our own creations since they are our failure to live up to what has been implanted within us." [2]

When adults in the spirit of Christ enter into challenging projects for community and world betterment and give the children a share in them, then the church will solve its problem of getting an adequate leadership. Too many children in the past have been trained to listen, to sit still, to sing, to give to a certain extent. As adults, they are results of their training. When the church guides children, from nursery age on, to be active participants in a Christian fellowship that is afire for God and goodness, then there will be no lack of people who are consecrated to our Lord's service and intelligent about it as well.

Some church activities for Primary children. Because of their natural interest in younger children, Primary children can carry out friendly activities for the nursery class. One

[2] Julius Seelye Bixler, "Must Religion Be Unreasonable?" *The American Scholar*, Summer 1939, p. 366.

second grade made a train out of cheese boxes, equipment really needed in the nursery room. They learned how to express their very real interest in nursery children in constructive ways.

These children received gifts from the nursery as well. One Christmas a row of little faces was seen outside the door of the Primary room. The nursery children had come to bring a tree they had trimmed for their friends. The nursery children were at home in the Primary Department. They called greetings to sisters and brothers and to playmates. They did not wish to leave.

Children in the kindergarten can have many friendly contacts with the Primary Department also. The Juniors may be looked to for help and included in friendly interchange. There is a warm, natural at-homeness about these experiences.

Another Primary Department gives a party for the kindergarten children every September. There is no problem of adjustment at promotion time. The kindergarten children know the Primary teachers personally, and the older children are already friends. They have been working together and visiting each other's rooms all during the year. When they come into the room, they already know where things are and how to work with the older children. Their adjustment is a delight.

If the older Primary children are in a two-grade group with the fourth grade, then there can be constant friendly interchange between the younger Primary and the other group. They can give parties for each other. They can share their work with each other. For instance, a third and a fourth grade (Lower Junior) arranged a worship program at Thanksgiving time. They invited the first and second grades to worship with them. When Palm Sunday came, one of the teachers in the Primary group was traveling in Florida. She sent a box of palm branches to the children. They dramatized the Palm Sunday story with great joy. Then they sent the box to the third and fourth grades, who used the palms in a processional during the morning worship service. They were delighted to have the branches as they added a final touch of reality to their singing.

Often parents' classes and the children's groups can work together on some enterprise which is too big for the children by themselves. Such an activity was the planning of a first-aid kit for a day nursery. The parents' class and the Primary group made a list of what was needed, determined what each group would give, reported to each other on progress; and finally, when the first-aid kit was carried to the day nursery, the members of the adult class took along a committee from the Primary group.

In planning such gifts for other groups the element of dramatic play should enter in. For example, one Primary group decided to send a box of equipment to a church center for Negro children. A list of the materials was made on a piece of wrapping paper with black crayon. It was hung on the wall. As the articles were brought, they were checked off the list. The children put them in the box many times before the final time for packing it. They played they were the train crew who carried the box to the center. They played they were nurses wrapping up a cut or swabbing a sore place. Through play their social horizons were widened.

Primary children not only receive visitors who come to share the missionary program of the church or the social program of the community with them, but they make trips and investigations. They visit the firehouse and learn how brave the men must be to take care of the families in the neighborhood. "For none of us liveth to himself" takes on new meaning in such a situation. In a crowded, downtown city church the children visit the florist for the breath of living beauty they may obtain from this trip. Children from a suburban church find some little nature spot near the church, perhaps a garden or a lane, and revel in evidences of the cycle of the seasons as they see them in this chosen place. They gather autumn leaves in the fall, feathery grasses in the summer. Their eyes are opened to the wonder of the world.

Children may take trips to community centers. These places are concrete examples of the loving care of religious people for people who have special needs. One Primary group visited a home for the aged on Easter. They carried them flowers, sang songs, and took a greeting card for each inmate of the home. A third grade was invited by a friendly Jewish family to visit their succoth, or booth.[3] Their own Thanksgiving time became far more meaningful to them after this trip. City children who are learning about "Out-of-door Life in Palestine" need trips to the country in order to compare life among the Hebrews and outdoor life today.

Participation in the missionary program. As they mature, children's social interests should include people of all the world. This is one of the great opportunities of the missionary program for children. First and second grades need to come in vivid, close contact with the work of the church in near-by places and to have first-hand experiences with this work. They live in a world of the here and now. They should see how the spirit of Christ is at work in their own world. But children in the third grade begin to be interested in life that is different from their own. So more extended missionary projects can be introduced in simple fashion.

The minister as pastor of children. The minister is the pastor of the entire congregation, both young and old. The Primary leader should see that the children have frequent and friendly contacts with their pastor, that he knows them personally, and that they are his friends. There was one minister who was tall and dignified, a scholar, and a fine administrator. There was never a time when this man was not available to his children. One of their first thoughts when they had carried out an interesting enterprise was, "Let's go find Dr. ——— and show it to him or tell him about it." Often the children would be seen talking to him in a friendly fashion outside the Primary room. When the third grade went into the church sanctuary, he was there to show them the Bible and to read one of their own memory passages, Psalms 100. He was their friend and their pastor, and the children appreciated him and trusted him.

Contacts with other persons. The children should have

³ Read Deut. 16:13-15 and Neh. 8 to learn of this October festival of gratitude.

contacts with other workers in the church. They should learn to express appreciation of the church secretary and to help her with simple tasks. The sexton in the church can have great influence on children. One sexton taught the Primary children as much as their own teacher. He was unfailingly patient and yet firm. He was ready to help them with all their large projects that they could not carry through themselves. For example, he helped them to build an Oriental house large enough for fifteen children to sit in at one time. Taking care of the room meant helping him. Abuse of church property was an unfriendly act toward this good friend.

The treasurer and the organist are friends that the children should know. They should learn how the church is supported and what is their part. One could go on indefinitely mentioning the contacts that Primary children should make with persons in the church. They should be as wide as friendship is wide and as natural as living together in the home; for the church should be a second home for Primary children, a place where they feel that they belong and where they find security, friendliness, and interesting work to do.

The children's friendly efforts should not be spasmodic. When children have learned to serve another group, these persons should become so real to them that they cannot drop them and become indifferent toward their continued welfare. In too many churches children give in piecemeal fashion at Thanksgiving and Christmas and forget all about the needs of the persons whom they are helping until another year has rolled around. The teacher can easily see the effect this practice would have on the child's sense of Christian responsibility for other persons, his respect for human personality.

Then there are the parents. How closely teachers should work with them.

Mutual sympathy and understanding between parents and teachers, and their close co-operation, is a third means of giving children security. When they are critical of each other, the child is affected in much the same way as when there is friction between father and mother. If one person or group to whom he feels that he belongs and in whom he has confidence is antagonistic, even silently, toward the other, his loyalty is divided, his foundations are unstable, his life is discontinuous. He needs instead the sense of school being an extension of home, of parents and teachers working wholeheartedly together, the school broadening and making more solid the security of home.[4]

Summary. In guiding the children in the fellowship of the church and in participation in the program of Christian people, certain principles should be followed:

1. Children's opportunities for brotherliness should develop as rapidly as the child matures. Children should not be plunged into complex, baffling problems when they are only growing familiar with their own social environment.

2. Children should learn at each level of their development to feel a sense of Christian responsibility for the welfare of people.

3. Friendly experiences within the group, within the church and community, and later on a larger scale, should be natural to children because they are natural to the teacher. Glover has a perfect phrase to describe what should be the quality of living together within the children's group in a Christian church. He used it to define the quality of living in the apostolic church: "Infinite love in ordinary intercourse." When the Christian church becomes a fellowship which has such a quality, our children learn the true meaning of "Thou shalt love thy neighbor as thyself," "Thou shalt love the Lord thy God."

4. Bible stories may be used to show how other Christian people have lived in love and friendliness. The children may hear stories of Jesus who was the friend of everyone.

5. The children themselves should invite the visitors. They should have a purpose in mind when they issue the invitation. Older Primary children can easily plan what they will ask a visitor who brings information. Younger Primary children will not organize their ideas so easily.

When children go on visits, they should be kept from patronizing "little poor children." One group of children were planning a surprise for a group at a Children's Home.

---

[4] Carleton Washburne, *A Living Philosophy of Education*, The John Day Co., 1940, p. 40.

Plans had been made with the workers at the home so that there would be no sense of superiority on the part of the visitors nor of inferiority on the part of the hosts. The children were first introduced to the play equipment. Then they went to see the pony. By the time they had come to the group of houses where the children lived, they were admiring the children and wishing they had such fine play equipment.[5]

When guiding contacts with another racial group, the leader should always emphasize the fundamental human likenesses and kinships rather than differences. There is sometimes a temptation to depend on differences for the sake of vividness.

6. The atmosphere of the Primary room has a great deal to contribute to the growth of children. If the teachers are friendly, interested in what the children suggest and do, and if there is a pleasant informal spirit of investigation and appreciation of each child's contribution, then the children have a fine basis for their growth in the fellowship of the church.

7. When an activity is started, it should be followed through. When children plan to help a day nursery, they should see their plans through to a successful conclusion. Again this is developing the sense of responsibility which is so necessary to the growth of Christian personality. The children learn to love their neighbors and to lose their lives in the larger life of the Christian fellowship.

8. Children should keep a record of their living and learning at church. Sometimes this may take the form of charts which the children will dictate and illustrate. The teacher writes these stories on a large sheet of wrapping paper or on construction paper. She uses black crayon or a speed ball pen and India ink. Children illustrate the stories. Poems or prayers or songs that the children make about the experience are still another form of record.

FOR FURTHER STUDY

*Hartshorne, Hugh. *Character in Human Relations.* New York: Charles Scribner's Sons, 1933.

[5] In contrast read Smith, *A Tree Grows in Brooklyn,* Harper & Bros., 1943, pp. 189-93.

Hockett, John A., and Jacobsen, E. W. *Modern Practices in the Elementary School.* Boston: Ginn & Co., 1938. Chap. II.

Hockett, Ruth M., editor. *Teacher's Guide to Child Development.* Sacramento: California State Board of Education, 1930. Chap. II. (Elementary.)

Lane, Robert H. *The Teacher in the Modern Elementary School.* Boston: Houghton Mifflin Co., 1941. Chap. V.

*Lee, J. Murray, and Lee, Doris M. *The Child and His Curriculum.* New York: D. Appleton-Century Co., 1940. Chap. VI.

McGavran, Grace W. *Creating Friendly Attitudes Through the Home.* New York: Friendship Press, 1941.

Mayer, Jane, and Sutherland, Miriam. *The Community.* New York: Progressive Education Association Service Center. (Pamphlet.)

Minor, Ruby. *Early Childhood Education.* New York: D. Appleton-Century Co., 1937. Chap. VII.

Mossman, Lois Coffey. *Principles of Teaching and Learning in the Elementary School.* Boston: Houghton Mifflin Co., 1929. Chaps. I, III.

Munkres, Alberta. *Which Way for Our Children.* New York: Charles Scribner's Sons, 1936. Chap. VIII.

Sherrill, Lewis J. *The Opening Doors of Childhood.* New York: The Macmillan Co., 1939. Chap. X.

Stewart, George. *The Church.* New York: Association Press, Hazen Foundation, 1938. Pp. 22-24, 49-56, 71-83; Chap. V.

*Washburne, Carleton. *A Living Philosophy of Education.* New York: The John Day Co., 1940. Chap. III.

Zyve, Claire T., compiler. *Growth Through School Living.* Washington: Association for Childhood Education, 1940. (Bulletin.)

FOR FURTHER ACTIVITY

1. After reviewing the work of your class for the past year, list all the opportunities that the children have had to participate in the program of the church.

2. What other plans could you introduce to give them a more important part in this program?

3. Ask your pastor to list for you ways that he could come into closer fellowship with the Primary children. Be prepared to make practical suggestions to him. Two suggestions are:

   a) The third grade could visit the church sanctuary to meet with him. He might explain to them interesting details of architecture and equipment. The children might sing for him.

   b) If your minister knows how to have fun with children, the children may plan a surprise party for him. Let them plan the games, bring the refreshments, and take care of the program.

4. Study the missionary education program of your church. What

is especially planned for Primary children? How do these plans integrate with suggested plans in your course of study?

5. What plans can you make to show friendliness to other groups of boys and girls within the church? List at least four ways.

6. How can the class for young married people and your group work together?

7. Relate two incidents of how you have helped your boys and girls to accept their part in the program of your church.

Chapter IX

GROWING RELIGIOUSLY THROUGH EXPERIENCES OF WONDER AND JOY

WONDER and joy help man to feel in harmony with the world. They make him sense through all his being the rhythms of the universe. So they are powerful emotions in nurturing the religious life. The Primary teacher should see that children are led to experience both of them. Early man felt himself a part of the world, as this quotation so strikingly tells us: "He was conscious of the world, and conscious of himself as a part of it, fitting into it, belonging to it, drawing strength and joy and existence from it. . . . He was conscious of an order which had never failed him." [1]

Teachers realize that wonder over the world has educative value for the child of today who has lost some of this natural at-homeness of earlier and more primitive man. "The wonder of the world should take hold of children. . . . In the words of Mr. Thomson, the sense of wonder is one of the saving graces of life; and if it dies, he says, one of the lights of life goes out." [2]

These two quotations lead into a consideration of another important kind of activity at church for Primary children. Every man and woman has a philosophy of life. Consciously or unconsciously he steers his course by it. "Out of the heart are the issues of life," said Jesus; and, indeed, out of a man's point of view come his decisions, just as likewise they change and remake that philosophy. It is the duty of the church to help children to see and value life from the Christian point of view. The experiences discussed in this chapter should help to establish it.

[1] Eleanor Dark, *The Timeless Land,* The Macmillan Co., 1941, p. 3.
[2] Bertha Stevens, *Child and Universe,* The John Day Co., 1931, p. 10.

The church that has a wise and well-rounded program for the Primary children will provide many experiences that lead them to sense that they have a home in the earth, that there is plan and orderly design in the universe, that all living things have a rhythm of growth and of life, and that this wonderful world is the provision of God the Father and Giver of Life.

Listening to stories or talks, looking at pictures, and singing songs will not give these fundamental religious experiences to Primary children. After all, these methods of teaching use experience at second hand. In stimulating wonder and joy Primary teachers must use first-hand experience. They should rely on some of the child's most powerful approaches to life —the keenness of his senses, his urge to find the meaning of life, his curiosity about his world. Children must have chances to wonder, to question, to see the rhythms and patterns of life. They must come gradually to look at this world from the Christian point of view.

Providing experiences of wonder. The room where Primary children meet should, if possible, provide living, growing things—goldfish, ferneries, terrariums, dish gardens, and flowers. There may be bulbs set in rocks and water. These living, growing things should be the children's own. They should help to provide them and care for them. Many a little child pauses with anticipation by the bulletin board to discover the task that lies ahead of him. If teachers could only remember how much children, like adults, want to be important, to gain a sense of worth from group recognition, they would surely see that there are things for children to look after at church.

One class of Primary children took care of a goldfish bowl. One Sunday they moved the bowl into the place for worship. "They're so pretty," said Marilyn with shining eyes. There was a time of silence while the children watched the fish. Then they sang a hymn of praise to God, the Giver of Life.

When bulbs are set, there should be careful, thoughtful planning. Just setting the bulbs does not make the experience a religious one. Children and teacher look at the brown, seemingly dead bulbs and wonder that they hold the power to grow and flower. The group watch the plants grow. They see how warmth, sunshine, water, and a firm support are necessary.

A group planted bulbs just before Christmas. One Sunday the teacher was speaking of the goodness of God in sending Jesus, his best gift to the world.

"Why do you talk about God?" asked one of the children. "He's dead."

"Yes," said another.

"Yes, I saw him," added a third child.

Questioning revealed that the children had seen a statue portraying the descent from the cross.

"The statue you saw was the way some people think of Jesus at Easter," said the teacher. "It was not meant to be God our Father. We do not make statues of him." Then she called the children's attention to the bulbs. Some of them already had swelling buds upon them. "Weren't they dead-looking at first!" she said. "Now see how full of life they are! The power that makes things live and grow, I call God," she added. "He is more alive and real to me than anything else in the world." Then she suggested that they sing "God Who Made the Earth." Without the experience of the bulbs, this teacher would have had little on which to base her teaching of the reality of a living God.

Teaching children out of doors. The children should not be shut up in a room at church, with a world to explore outside. Some fortunate churches can provide a small plot where the children may have a garden. There must be careful planning, responsibility carried faithfully, and many chances to use the flowers in the room and to share them. Poems, songs, prayers, may be used along with the activity. Children sense the mystery of growth and learn the patience of faith as they bury bulbs in the fall and wait for new life. There is the joy of discovery of awakening life and the fun of sharing.

Children may learn to see wonder in an open field when a spiritually minded adult helps to open their eyes. Feathery grasses and delicate wild flowers, like Queen Anne's lace, can make a Mount Horeb of this place; for the children will feel:

> . . . Earth's crammed with heaven,
> And every common bush afire with God.

Providing release from tension. There was once a little boy who had a serious emotional tension. He scowled, was unfriendly with the other children, and was always tense. One Sunday the teacher took a Bermuda hibiscus flower to church. She had an inexpensive magnifying glass. The little boy looked long at the blossom, its color, its pattern, its form. Finally he slowly relinquished it to another child. "That's the most beautiful thing I ever saw," he said, eyes shining, body relaxed, completely unself-conscious for the first time. Here was a child who found his better self through wonder.

Observing rhythms in nature. Primary children gain a sense of security from observing such processes as the egg-bird cycle and that of caterpillar-butterfly. Day and night are a rhythm, and the child may swing in tune to the change. The cycle of the seasons is another evidence of the order of the universe. Children who have made a frieze of the seasons or dramatized a song that celebrates the year's changes, wonder of the snow crystal, red and gold of autumn, spring's flush of life, summer's drowsy richness, have a growing realization of the purpose and wisdom that guide the world.

Older Primary children can understand how even sudden spells of cold and ice in spring are predictable in a temperate climate. Over a period of years man can expect sudden chills to come in early spring or fall, and floods in flood areas.

Helping children to record experience. Children should make records of their experiences of wonder, for they gain added understanding from trying to organize mentally what has happened. Of course, older Primary children are more helped by such a plan than the younger ones who have less ability to stand off and look at what is happening to them.

Not all records are made in words. Some of the best ones made by Primary children take other forms. Making blueprints, for example, is a delightful form of record for Primary children. The modern child is scientific enough to want to understand something of the process. In all his nature work he is helped best to wonder by an avoidance of any sentimental or vague handling of facts. The world itself is wonderful enough for the child who is guided to see it with understanding and appreciative eyes and to think of it as the handiwork of God.

Children like to keep a record of their observations of signs of spring or of fall. A large chart to which records are gradually added can mean much to the children. "I seen a robin. He was fat," wrote Jean on the teacher's typewriter. Then she posted her slightly ungrammatical notice of a world-shaking event.

The children like also to record their experiences by making collections. If there is a nature table, they naturally make contributions to it. One group made it a practice to bring nature objects and other objects back with them to help tell the story of vacation time.

Another class made a collection of seed to show how they were scattered. The verse from the Psalms, "This is the Lord's doing; it is marvelous in our eyes," was a perfect expression of the children's feeling about the collection.

A hymn can help children to summarize and record experiences of wonder. One group were finding beauty in the out-of-doors, making blueprints, making large pictures of their vacation experiences, and writing stories about them. The hymn "All Things Bright and Beautiful," sung and illustrated, was a perfect expression for the children.

Any good Primary course of study will offer many opportunities for activities that lead to wonder. This book mentions only a few. The wise Primary teacher regards them as useful, full of religious value, and suitable in religious teaching. She knows where children live most truly, how their philosophy of life develops, and what is basic to the experience of worship for younger children.

Not all the wonder of the Primary child grows out of his contacts with the natural world. Sometimes his experiences with people lead him to find his way to the God of life also. One Sunday a teacher was discussing the gift of life with the children. They talked about the trees, flowers, and birds, about the animals and the fish in the sea. Just then a little child of three ran into the room. She was looking for a sister; but because she knew the superintendent well, she ran up to her and leaned against her. The superintendent looked down at the little child and then at her children. There was tenderness in their eyes, and wonder too. So the conversation developed about the wonderful gift of life to people. The group talked about the strength to run, the wonderful sense of being rested in the morning. They thought of all creation and of themselves as part of the work of God. The worship time that Sunday was one of the high points in both teacher's and children's experience.

The festivals. The festivals often stimulate and nurture the child's wonder. He watches the fat red candle burn; he smells the spice of evergreens. He hears the bells ring out for Christmas, and the organ play. He sings the carols through which men express their wondering joy over Advent. All of these church experiences can be times of worshipful wonder, joy, and understanding, as well as just sensory experiences, for the Primary child.

Through using simple social and sense experiences as a foundation, first meanings in religion begin. This poem shows wise guidance in a first introduction to religion through wonder, joy in human relations, and tenderness:

RELIGION

"What is religion?" asked the six-year-old.
I tried to answer: "It's the way you feel
When lovely things are near you—sunshine's gold;
Or happy music from the bells that peal
In church; or soft cloud shadows slowly creeping;
Or stars. . . ." He stopped me there. "I know, I guess—
Like looking at the baby when he's sleeping.
Is that the way you mean?" And I said, "Yes." [3]

[3] Eleanor Graham, *This Week Magazine*. Copyright, 1942, by the United Newspapers Magazine Corporation. The poem appears also in Miss Graham's *For These Moments*, Stephen Daye Press, Battleboro, Vermont.

Joy and the religion of children. Joy and religion should go hand in hand for both child and adult. We moderns have vitiated the word "joy" by confusing it with pleasurable excitement and overstimulated nerves until the good word has lost its real meaning. Ernest Dimnet [4] tells us that the early Christian expected great joy as a normal accompaniment of his experience of the living Christ. In fact, joy was a proof of the coming of the Holy Spirit. The Bible is filled with the joy of men who have served and known God. "The joy of the Lord is your strength," and "Rejoice in the Lord alway," we may quote. The religion of the Christian centers in the joyful triumph over the cross, the symbol of man's most ruthless materialistic brutality. A modern poet has caught the old wisdom of the Bible; for John Masefield writes, "The days that make us happy make us wise."

Our little children need many experiences of joy that are associated with the church and with the life of good will and friendliness. There should be laughter in a Primary department, not excitable, strident, mirthless laughter, but the joy that comes when people like each other, like to be together, enjoy learning together and engaging together in worthy thinking and service. In this sense, joy, like wonder and fellowship, should be a part of every experience in the Primary group. In this book they are only set apart the better to discuss them.

I SAW JOY

I saw joy in the face of a little child today,
The real joy that makes me happy
To say I work with him.
It was his birthday and
We sang a song for him;
It made him smile and smile,
And let out little sighs
That seemed to crowd his chest;
And I said, "Seven,

4 *What We Live By*, Simon and Schuster, 1932, pp. 282-84.

Is it, Richard?" and he
Looked up and nodded yes,
And turned away again,
While we clapped out the years.[5]

Joy through music. There are no more joyful experiences
than those that music gives to Primary children. The reader
is referred to Chapter VI for a discussion of guidance
through music.

Joy through literature and art. Experiences with literature are discussed in Chapter V. The arts and religious
growth is dealt with in Chapter VII. These are also joyous
experiences that nurture religious learning.

Joy through play and dramatic play. The real life of
the Primary child is play. Every Primary room should reflect
this fact. It should influence the teachers' planning and relations with their children. At Christmas time one combined
first- and second-grade group set up a very simple crèche on
top of a sturdy table. It was ready early in the month. All
during December the children played the Christmas stories.
As they told the story, they moved the figurines around. The
more the teachers stayed out of the situation, the freer and
more poetic the play became. This is a form of dramatic
play that Primary children follow constantly in their free
play. They use it at church when they have freedom. Sometimes there was a little group who played the Christmas stories; sometimes a single child was absorbed by the crèche.
Several children played the stories for their parents after
church school. As they came with their children to Bethehem,
it was good to watch the adults' faces. Often the children
sang a Christmas song as they played the story.

When the children give presents to some other group, they
like to play with these presents themselves. One group made
up a box of books for a center. They read many of the books
themselves. They played that they were the children who received the box and imagined how much they enjoyed the
stories. No book went into the box that they themselves
did not like.

[5] Josephine Chero, *in Childhood Education*, April, 1942, p. 361.

One year a second grade packed a supply kit for a migrant center. The plan was initiated by placing a large box on the table and imagining all its surprise at being at church school, and its joy in having a part in the plans for the migrant center. "It would have clapped its hands with joy, but it had no hands to clap. It would have smiled, but it has no mouth." The box's personality became so real that the children drew "a mouth to smile" and "hands to clap" on the box. They felt a sense of personal inadequacy for the box until they did. They packed the box in their own character and unpacked it as children at the migrant center. "This will help my hurt hand," Jack was heard to say, iodine bottle in hand.

The children in a third grade made a cart for the kindergarten. Not the least of the joy was in taking the little children for rides and riding in it themselves. Play, imaginative and sympathetic thinking, social living, are nearly one thing for Primary children.

Joy through dramatization. The first dramatization by Primary children is quite like the dramatic play that has just been described. Children dramatize when they are thoroughly familiar with stories that have strong action and vivid characterization. The teacher moves slowly and does not tell a new story each session. To linger over familiar material, to gain new insight into its meaning, to arrange it in new relationships to use it in worship—this is what genuine learning requires.

Suppose children have grown familiar with a story that has strong and simple action. If they are young children, they will play it spontaneously. If they are in third grade, they usually organize the dramatization and play with a purpose in view. The leader tells the story while younger children act it out without suggestion; or, after this procedure at first, they add a simple dialogue. It is doubtful whether young children dramatize easily for an audience.

With older children the leader asks, "What happens in this story?" She writes down the acts as the children analyze the story. She helps them to master action step by step. "How will you show where this story takes place?" The children may decide to paint the backdrops on large sheets of newsprint or wrapping paper. Or the boys and girls will set up simple scenery in the room. A group of chairs together may be the thicket out of which the bear came to attack David's flock, for example.

Then the children will probably work out simple costumes. One group were constantly playing stories. They brought all their properties from home. Teachers are much more realistic than their pupils. Children get good effect from sketchy details and imagination.

Children have no self-consciousness about the parts they play if the dramatization is truly their own. The writer recalls a group of boys in third grade who made willingly and sincerely a most realistic herd of sheep for David.

One Primary group decided to write and play a simple operetta of the Baby Moses. They found a poem in one of the children's folders. It was:

> We have made a basket,
>   Miriam and I,
> Put you safely in it,
>   Smiling at the sky.
>
> River tides will rock you,
>   River reeds will sing,
> Bulrushes will hide you,
>   Safe from Egypt's king.
>
> When the princess finds you,
>   You need have no fear;
> She will love and keep you
>   Through the happy year.
>
> Mother's love is round you,
>   Sister watches there;
> Reeds and rivers singing,
>   "You are in God's care." [*]

"We could write the music," said Kendall. "I hear the first line this way." He sang it with confidence. The rest of the children liked his phrase, so the teacher wrote it down. Slowly but surely the rest of the music grew. Then the children de-

[*] Edith Lombard Squires, "Lullaby for Baby Moses," *Picture Story Paper,* May 1, 1938.

cided what parts they would need. The "mother" sang the first four lines, then the "River Tides" the next; the "River Reeds" the next. A chorus sang the next two lines.

The "Princess" sang the next four lines, the "Mother" the next, "Miriam" the next; and the "Reeds" and the "River" completed the song. The children worked out this allotment themselves.

Then they painted a large backdrop of a river with palm trees and rushes. As they worked they looked in books to find out what to paint.

The group decided on and supplied the costumes. The Reeds held cattails in their arms. The River was robed in blue. "Is this a good enough crown for Egypt's King?" Philip asked as he produced a very ornate one made of gold paper. His brother, who was studying about Egypt at public school, had made it. Even the basket and the doll for the infant Moses were supplied by the children. Better one Bible story a month that is really lived and enjoyed than four unsuitable ones jumbled together in hazy fashion and vaguely understood.

Children dramatize easily when they have background for it. One group had a large Palestinian house 6 feet by 6 feet by 5 feet in one corner of the room. They sat on its roof, imagined that they were under a deep blue Palestinian night sky, and had a moment of joyous worship through saying and singing verses from the Psalms. They used the house to play the Sabbath meal and such stories as the Woman of Shunem and Elisha. Another group had a tent on the church lawn. In it they sat at times during the sessions of a vacation church school and wondered about the world, the beginning of things, the meaning of life. They imagined that they were Hebrew shepherds. Some of the Bible's answers to age-old questions were introduced.

Another group had a big Bible six feet high built in front of an extra entrance into the room that the leaders could well do without. It was covered with black cambric. When the front opened, it was like opening a book. The children posed Children of the Bible. They wrote the stories on large charts.

They chose a child to read the chart while another posed the story within the big "book." A sheet made the page of the book, the backdrop. Of course, one child opened and closed the Bible. There were the young Moses, the little King Josiah, and so on. But, alas, there were more children in the group than in the Bible. "Surely there were many children in the crowd who welcomed Jesus on Palm Sunday," the teacher suggested. "We will," the children said with a little whoop of joy. So there was no audience except some adult friends. Who wants to be an onlooker anyway when he can be a participant? Only the mature who are limited by their grown-upness are spectators of life. None of these departments had expanded sessions. The teachers secured their equipment themselves, but they knew how to make the most of what they had.

Joy through choric speaking. The beauty of the spoken word is becoming more evident to people, thanks to John Masefield and his Scottish group. Instead of singing, children enjoy saying together lovely poetry of a rhythmic quality. Older groups divide the voices into light and dark, but this is too pretentious a grouping for young children. Probably the Psalms have too complex a rhythm for Primary children, though a third- and fourth-grade group has used Psalms 100 and Psalms 24 beautifully in this way. The teacher should not regard this as a "recitation," drill on it, or try to make the children little mimics by forcing her interpretation of the poem on them.

Some younger Primary children used "What the Church Bells Say" [7] in choric speaking. The children, in three groups, were the bells. Of course, the point of this piece is that all the bells keep the same beat.

"In Little Bethlehem" proves a lovely poem for choric speaking at Christmas. "Cherries," by Walter de la Mare, was used with a unit on elemental needs. "A Letter Is a Gypsy Elf," by Annette Wynne, is fine with a missionary-education emphasis.

Very little method is needed in choric speaking with young

---

[7] Alberta Munkres, *I Wonder*, The Abingdon Press, 1930.

children. The teacher should have a good sense of the beat of the poem that she may help the children to sense it. She may make a copy of the poem on a large sheet of paper. She uses manuscript writing, with letters large and well-spaced. She may use a black crayon for this work. She lets the children live with the poem and see themselves how it may be spoken. In a little while they do it beautifully.

Summary. Experiences of wonder and of joy help children to grow religiously because they help them to gain a working philosophy of life that is Christlike and to live according to this philosophy. They help children to have a rich, joyous, natural, and varied experience of learning. They associate happiness and interest with the work and life at the church. This early zest for the church experience has a large influence on the individual's attitude to the church throughout life and on his skill in church worship.

Experiences of wonder and of joy also help children to grow religiously because they recognize the world in which children learn and think—the strong sensory experience, the play approach, the pleasant group life, the active quality of child living and learning. Primary children learn best through such definite, concrete, and emotionally fulfilling experiences.

FOR FURTHER STUDY

Brown, Corinne. *Creative Drama in the Lower School.* New York: D. Appleton-Century Co., 1929.

Forest, Ilse. *The School for the Child from Two to Eight.* Boston: Ginn & Co., 1935. Pp. 186-89.

Garrison, Charlotte G. *Permanent Play Materials for Young Children.* New York: Charles Scribner's Sons, 1926.

——— *Science Experiences for Little Children.* New York: Charles Scribner's Sons, 1939.

Hall, Mary Ross. *Children Can See Life Whole.* New York: Association Press, 1941. Chap. VI.

*Lee, J. Murray, and Lee, Doris M. *The Child and His Curriculum.* New York: D. Appleton-Century Co., 1940. Pp. 569-71, 577-84.

Rasmussen, Carrie. *Choral Speaking for Speech Improvement.* Boston: Expression Co., 1939.

Science and the Young Child. Washington: Association for Childhood Education. (This pamphlet is especially valuable for its suggested activities and sources for supplies.)

*Stevens, Bertha. *Child and Universe*. New York: The John Day Co., 1931.

—— *How Miracles Abound*. New York: The John Day Co., 1941.

FOR FURTHER ACTIVITY

1. Check through the unit you are teaching to see what experiences you find that likely will lead to wonder and joy. How many of these suggestions have you used? What were your results?

2. How would you explain to a mother what value growing things have in a Primary room?

3. How do you evaluate this leader's statement? "After all, children can't do much, and they are messy. My teachers and I prefer to look after the flowers in our room ourselves." Give reasons for your judgment.

4. What would you do if these incidents happened in your room at church? Can you see how the departments where they did happen could use them to guide religious growth?

a) A boy arrives with a jar containing frogs' eggs.

b) A child brings a cocoon. In the midst of a story one child notices that the moth is emerging.

c) A boy runs into the room. He is quite excited. He lives across the street from the church. He almost shouts, "We have new baby chicks. We have new baby chicks."

d) John announces to the teacher, eyes big with wonder, "There is a new baby at our house." The other children grow excited.

e) Frank announces, "A robin has made a nest over the screen door at the park house. Will you take us to see it?"

f) The windows of the Primary room are covered with frost crystals.

5. Tell how a birthday can be made an experience of joy for a Primary child and be given religious meaning.

Chapter X

PRIMARY LEARNING AND WORSHIP

What worship is. Worship may be described as the consciousness of God's presence that lends new value and meaning to daily life and to efforts for human good. It increases one's power and desire to find the best possible solutions to life's problems and to follow them. It gives comfort and peace in the light of one's best, and forgiveness and release for a regretted worst. It helps to increase one's sense of the mystery of life. Like electricity, it has energizing quality and so makes the worshiper conscious of the life eternal that is already his. For group worship there may be added to this definition a feeling of "togetherness," of common purposes and exaltations, common confession and reconsecration. Every chapter of this book has shown children worshiping as a natural part of their living at church. This discussion of worship is set apart merely for purposes of study.

Worship among Primary children. Thoughtful leaders of Primary children ask themselves how much of group worship is possible for children and how it may be achieved. They know that ability to worship in a group is one of the skills in living that develop with guidance and maturity. The teacher asks herself also, How may I help individuals with problems of worship?

Once most Primary departments thought of worship as a worship service. It was assigned a certain part of the morning hour. The superintendent was responsible for this part of the program. It had little or no connection with the class period that usually followed it. This plan is gradually being abandoned by resourceful leaders who realize how the Primary boys and girls worship. Primary children do not have such a command over themselves that they worship just in a formal service or at a special time. Primary leaders are trying to find out what are the foundations for child worship and to supply them in their Primary rooms. Probably most Primary departments that serve three grades together will continue to plan for a time when the entire group is together. Opportunities to worship will be given to the children at this time; but fellowship, planning, and worship training will be associated with it. It will be a flexible conference and worship plan. This is the way that worship is most likely to come to Primary children—in the midst of group living. The leaders will see that the entire session is unified at this time. They will use the devotional materials from the class groups to help them worship. This in turn will supply motive for learning in the class and lend greater meaning to class-work. Superintendent and teachers will plan together so that such oneness of experience is possible.

The teachers will be very much concerned that there be experiences of worship in their classes. If possible, there will be opportunities sometimes for one class or for a grade to worship alone.

One large Primary department is recalled where each grade had the room entirely to itself every two months. The other two grades planned trips for this Sunday. A schedule was worked out so these trips were a part of the regular class learning. Sometimes the third grade went on a trip. A great deal of thinking needs still to be done on the subject of group worship for young children, and no one can be dogmatic. Rather careful experimentation has brought to light some findings about the worship of Primary children that can be shared by all teachers.

Foundations for worship. What are the characteristics of child nature that are basic to a child's worship? The first one is the result of the child's desire to understand his world and to find meaning in life. The child must know in order to build his own philosophy of life. Since worship adds clearness to his understanding of his world, this search for reality is one of the natural foundations for worship. Some workers think that a little child's wonder as he faces the world is a primary mystical experience and that he is more fitted to worship than an adult. Other workers consider this wonder more akin to credulity than to worship. They think that, properly guided, it is one of the foundations for worship on the level of the Christian experience and that ability to worship as a Christian gradually grows.

Probably the child's ability to worship grows best when he is allowed to wonder and to be quiet. Children's leaders should avoid the idea that they can explain the deeps of life easily to children. Many parents and teachers within the last decades have tried to explain everything religious and thus bring religion to a dead level. Do they not wish, instead, to find an opportunity to guide this sense of wonder of the young child into the spiritual experiences of the adult who is mature religiously?

The other basis for worship helps teachers to see the tremendous importance of group living. Children are able really to participate in group worship to the extent that they are ready emotionally and socially to enter happily into normal group experiences and to lose themselves there. This is the gradually developing sense of "otherness" of which Dean Sperry writes. The child psychologists would say that as the child becomes socialized he is better able to enter into group worship. Growing from complete self-centeredness to a regard for his fellows and their worth, the child begins to experience the spirit of God moving within the group. Unless this socialization takes place, it is problematic whether even an adult enters into group worship.

Informal worship. Need for greater informality in worship is apparent to many Primary teachers. Some churches have solved the problem of informality in worship for younger Primary children by organizing on the grade or department unit plan. There is no break between class and worship experience. Activities chosen by the pupils themselves and carried out in their own groups form a natural basis for moments of worship within the smaller group and in the entire group at the time of conference. The unity, so essential to worship as a climax of experience, is provided for. Older Primary children need both formal and informal worship.

Some leaders of small groups regard them as merely activity groups. They do not sense when the climax in worship may come.

A group in a second grade was working on a unit on the church. The children chose to make a bulb garden in a sheltered corner of the church lawn. They wished to have something pretty to share when spring came. The leader and the group talked about the plan to set the bulbs away safely for the winter. The leader recited the poem "The Little Brown Bulbs." [1] When spring came, the children talked about who should be invited to see the garden. They sang joyously the response "I Will Sing to the Lord as Long as I Live," and this became a genuine worship experience. Yet that leader might have helped the group merely to plant bulbs!

A third grade was absorbed in its part in a Community Chest drive. The children studied Hole's picture "He Healed Many That Were Sick" and heard the story "The Busy Day at Capernaum." They sang "A Song of Service." They chose the Moffatt translation of Matthew 25:40 to learn. They prayed to thank God for the kindliness of Jesus to all people and to express their joy that friends of Jesus might carry on his work.

One group was making toys for a children's home. The leader realized that a deep personal interest in the children at the home had developed. After conversation the boys and girls very naturally made and used a prayer. They asked that these children in whom they were so much interested might never be cold, hungry, or afraid. Then one of the boys, remembering the boys at the home, added, "And we do want them to have a lot of fun."

Sometimes reporting from small group or class leads to just such moments of worship. In examining some seeds that a group was collecting as evidence of God's care, a third

[1] Margaret Prescott Montague. Quoted in *Graded Courses, Primary Blue Folder*, Course II, No. 24.

grade swung into a genuine worship experience by singing "This Is My Father's World."

One Primary department was working on "Friendliness at Church." The first grade was busy with plans for finding friendliness. The second grade was "working at church." The third grade was learning how friends of Jesus work together through the church. One Sunday the first grade showed its picture—"Jesus, the Friend of Everyone." The second grade dramatized the story of Barnabas. The third grade sang "Friends of Jesus." The prayer was an expression that fitted into what each grade was doing. The Primary superintendent and the teachers must plan in their regular meetings for group worship like this. They must be on the alert to use every opportunity that presents itself.

Formal worship and Primary children. The question is sometimes asked, "Do Primary children ever enjoy formal services of worship?" Surely they do when they purpose to have such services. A Primary group thoroughly enjoyed a most formal service at Thanksgiving. They had planned it, and much living and learning had preceded it. They used their own materials in it. Services of worship in the church sanctuary may have real stateliness and formality and mean much to Primary children, provided they have a sense of belonging to the larger group and also that they have some familiarity with the service. Their part in it must be brief. Activities like those described in Chapter VIII may help to build this sense of belonging; and careful training in materials of worship, for example, learning a hymn, gives the sense of familiarity.

Training in worship materials and techniques should never be neglected. For example, there may be special times to learn hymns. This training is not worship, but it should be provided for regularly. Often, in the midst of it, moments of genuine worship will come. Even if they do not, this guidance safeguards the children from missing chances to worship because they are inarticulate. Class teachers should teach the materials for worship in the course of study.

Genuine group worship comes to primary children only when group feeling is developed through play, through working together for common good, through group discovery, through study. Worship grows out of living and is its climax. Worship enriches life, that nobler living and better fellowship may result. The test of effectiveness is not what splendid programs children's leaders may devolop, how well they may choose emphases and find materials, but what group living they have provided that lends vitality to those programs and affords a reason for their being. What happens to the child and to the group life as a result of the worship experience?

Times of quietness. Children need times of quietness, for they contribute to their religious growth. This is especially true at holiday seasons, when the children become tired and overexcited. Their voices are shrill, and they are often irritable with each other. At such a time the pianist may play very softly music that is soothing. The children may sit quietly in their chairs and listen. The music should be very brief, and the entire experience should last for only a very few minutes. Often a noisy group of children becomes a quiet and calm one because of such an experience. Sometimes the leader may end the time of quietness with a spoken prayer, sometimes with a worshipful song such as "Lord of the Sunlight." At other times she may speak quietly to the children. Such an experience helps a child to resolve his tensions and feel at peace within himself and with the other children.

There is another kind of quietness that often leads to worship. This is the experience of wonder. There is no comment by the teacher on what has happened. The group sits quietly for a brief moment, or perhaps the pianist plays a few measures of some appropriate music. At Christmas time one Primary group drew the curtains and lighted a large, fat red candle. The children sat in the darkness and watched the candle flicker. They smelled the spiciness of branches of balsam and pine that decorated the room. The pianist played quietly "Silent Night." At first there was stillness in the group. Nobody knew when the children began to sing. It seemed natural to go on with their own song of praise, "I

Will Sing to the Lord as Long as I Live." [2] It seems that the Christmas season is the only time that justifies the use of candles in a Primary group. If they are lighted at other times, the child is so absorbed by the experience of watching the flickering light that he probably does not hear anything that is said. Used at Christmas time and in the way that has been suggested, the lighted candle becomes an experience of wonder and of joy.

Giving. When children learn to give for purposes which they understand and which are part of their entire experience in the Primary room, the sharing becomes a genuine act of worship. Such offerings should not be merely of money, although the giving of money can be a genuine act of worship for Primary children. There was once a Primary group who learned about a minister who needed a trailer so that he could "carry the church" to children in one of the far-flung sections of the United States. A little trailer hitched to a tiny automobile was placed on the table before the group. The children played with it. They used it as a bank. They imagined the little children on the prairies entering the trailer, how they enjoyed the music, and how they learned to work and sing and worship together. Giving money for this trailer church was a most joyous experience in worship for these children.

Another group of younger Primary children decided to send a "mitten tree" to a church center. The activity started one cold December morning. As the children hurried into the room, the leader called attention to a pair of red mittens that lay upon the table.

"I wore them this morning," she said, "because it was so cold. They kept my hands warm."

The children immediately showed their mittens and tried on hers because they liked their bright red.

"Aren't they warm!" said the teacher. Then later, when the right time had come, she told of how she had seen a little boy in town that week who had no mittens and whose hands were blue from the cold.

"Why doesn't his mother buy him some?" one child asked.

[2] Edith Lovell Thomas, *Sing, Children, Sing*, Abingdon-Cokesbury Press, 1939

"But wait," said one of the teachers. "This is how much money his mother makes each week. His father is ill."

The group found that there was not enough money for food and clothes and shelter, much less for mittens. Then the suggestion was made that they could send the mittens. The leader told about a center where the children often came with cold hands. The director of this center was invited to tell about her children.

One of the teachers brought a small tree the next Sunday. The pair of red mittens the leader had worn was hung on it. One of the other children had brought a pair of mittens. They were added, and so from Sunday to Sunday throughout December the tree grew gayer and gayer. The children wrote a poem that started

> Did you ever hear of a mitten tree
> With yellow and red and blue?
> It is as gay as it can be;
> It stands there ready for you.

They put on and took off the mittens. One Sunday a little girl put a pair of yellow mittens on her hands. She looked up into the teacher's eyes, her own shining. "Warm," she said; and the teacher nodded without speaking. This was an experience of worship for a child in a privileged situation. Some of the prayers that grew out of the experience were sincere ones. The children sang "When Each One Has a Secret" with joy, and the leader spoke of how happy she was that her group had an opportunity to make the world seem kinder at Christmas time.

The third grade of another Primary department invited the first and second grades to learn some of their carols. The second grade asked the third grade to help plan and prepare gifts for minister, sexton, and church secretary. The first grade made a Santa Claus chimney by covering a paper box with red crepe paper. They invited the other children to have a part in filling it for a day nursery. Class work and worship were unified without difficulty in that department.

When the giving of money is done in leisurely fashion,

the money may sometimes be counted just for the joy of counting and to see how nearly the sum meets the need. Then the giving is a real act of worship, because the child thinks beyond himself. He feels himself a co-worker with God in meeting others' needs and, to the best of his ability, he learns to live in loving charity with others. Giving should go on in class as well as department for the sake of timid children. The money may then be turned over to the secretary.

The giving of articles should also be a part of the child's experience, and play with these articles is an excellent preparation for worship. In fact, one wonders whether it is not actually part of the child's worship.

Prayer life. The prayer life was discussed on page 31.

Worship and children. Leaders may realize that an experience that is vivid, colorful, happy, and friendly is what nurtures the religious life of Primary children. Class teachers as well as superintendents are responsible for the worship of the children. Worship lifts a life to a climax of reality and beauty. It is life itself, fellowship with the God whom one is learning to love and serve.

FOR FURTHER STUDY

*Coe, George A. *What Is Christian Education?* New York: Charles Scribner's Sons, 1929. Pp. 122 ff.

Munkres, Alberta. *Which Way for Our Children?* New York: Charles Scribner's Sons, 1936.

Perkins, Jeanette E. *As Children Worship.* Boston: The Pilgrim Press, 1936.

Powell, Marie Cole. *Guiding the Experience of Worship.* New York: Abingdon-Cokesbury Press, 1935.

Sperry, Willard L. *Reality in Worship.* New York: The Macmillan Co., 1925.

*Vogt, Von Ogden. *Modern Worship.* New Haven: Yale University Press, 1927.

FOR FURTHER ACTIVITY

1. List in parallel columns, from your course of study, songs, Bible verses, poems, and stories of a worshipful character that belong together. How many of them are used in your Primary department? Compare your list with the lists made by teachers in the other two grades. How do they fit together?

2. List ten of the songs that you plan to teach.

3. List about six or seven important Bible verses that you plan to teach.

4. List four poems with worshipful emphasis.

5. Make a chart for the department containing the choices of teachers in all three grades for the lists suggested in 2, 3, and 4 above. This is a work chart of worship materials for the year. Why is it also a good memorization chart?